BAKED
to
ORDER

60 SWEET AND SAVORY RECIPES WITH VARIATIONS FOR EVERY CRAVING

RUTH MAR TAM
Creator of Cook Til Delicious

PHOTOGRAPHY BY DIANA MURESAN

PAGE STREET
PUBLISHING CO.

PAGE STREET
PUBLISHING CO.

Distributed by Macmillan, sales in Canada by The Canadian Manda Group.

24   23   22   21   20   1   2   3   4   5

ISBN-13: 978-1-64567-194-7

ISBN-10: 1-64567-194-1

Library of Congress Control Number: 2019957336

Cover and book design by Laura Benton for Page Street Publishing Co.

Photography by Diana Muresan

Printed and bound in the United States

TO MARCUS, HANNAH, AND ISABELLE—
THE BEST THINGS I'VE EVER BAKED.

contents

introduction

I first started baking out of boredom.

It was early February; I had just gotten married and moved from my hometown of Seattle to Toronto. For the first time in my adult life I wasn't studying or working full-time. Instead, while waiting for my work eligibility to kick in, I was "funemployed." If it had been spring or summer, maybe I would have gone for long walks or taken up gardening. But it was smackdab in the middle of a chilly Canadian winter, so staying inside next to a warm oven seemed like the better option. And there, in a small basement apartment with an old oven and a few mismatched pots and pans, my baking journey began.

Bake by bake—and with a lot of reading and YouTubing in between—I learned how to make flaky pie crusts and decorate layer cakes. I got bit by the sourdough bug and built a starter, which is bubbling away on the counter as I type. When winters rolled around, I'd try my hand at laminating dough for homemade croissants and Danishes. Somewhere along the way, my blog cooktildelicious.com was born so I could keep track of recipes.

A lot has changed since those early baking experiments in that basement apartment. Now, there are three little kids running around our modest suburban kitchen, eager to add sprinkles to everything and lick the frosting beaters. These days I bake not to beat boredom, but to both nourish loved ones and express creativity. However, with less time to learn new techniques, I've worked more on reimagining tried-and-true recipes with a "bake smarter, not harder" approach. If you have a few solid base recipes in your back pocket, you don't need to reinvent the wheel each time you want to create something different. Simply swapping out the mix-ins in your favorite cookies or switching up the filling and frosting of your go-to chocolate cake can transform a familiar recipe into something fresh. It's a new kind of creative challenge, but one that's truly exciting with endless possibilities.

This cookbook is my collection of sweet and savory recipes, from banana bread to brownies to sourdough bread to chicken pot pie. They range from simple everyday bakes with Flaky Buttermilk Biscuits, Infinitely Riffable (page 24) and Spelt and Honey Oatmeal Raisin Cookies (page 30) to ambitious weekend projects such as Mushroom Diamond Pastries (page 143) and Sourdough Cinnamon Rolls (page 118). There are Coconut Cocktail Buns (page 103) and Curry Beef Puffs (page 136) inspired by my Asian heritage; and Bourbon Butter Tarts (page 69) and No-Bake Nanaimo Bars (page 38) in tribute to my adopted country of Canada. Every recipe also includes variations— flour swaps, filling and frosting alternatives, different shaping techniques, flavor profile tweaks, and mix-in suggestions—to whet your creativity and satisfy every craving. There's also a chapter on repurposing leftovers so that nothing goes to waste.

I hope these recipes will inspire you to break out your rolling pin and preheat the oven. I hope the pages of this book will be butter-stained and the margins filled with notes on how you've made these recipes your own. And most of all, I hope you'll find joy in baking these recipes and that your delicious creations will bring smiles and delight to you and yours.

Ruth Tam

how to use this book

READ THE WHOLE RECIPE

Before you take out any ingredients or turn on the oven, read the entire recipe from start to finish. This will give you a good idea of what to expect, what ingredients and equipment are needed, and help you plan your time accordingly. Some of these recipes can be finished in an hour, but others have multiple elements or require lengthy rising times. If there are any processes or terms that are new to you, take time to understand them before you get to that step in the recipe—this will make the whole baking process much more enjoyable!

WEIGH YOUR INGREDIENTS

Whenever anyone asks me for tips to improve their baking, my first question is, "Do you own a kitchen scale?" There are many reasons why I love baking by weight, but the main one is consistency. Volume measurements, particularly for essential ingredients such as flour, sugar, and butter, are notoriously inconsistent—ask ten people to measure out a cup of flour and each of those cups will likely differ in weight depending on who's measuring, how compressed the flour is in the bag, whether the flour was spooned into the measuring cup or the cup was dipped directly into the bag, and so on. But 100 grams of flour is 100 grams of flour, no matter who is measuring. Baking requires precision for consistent results, and using weight measurements whenever possible is one way to instantly improve your accuracy.

I do generally use tablespoons and teaspoons for small measurements (e.g., for leaveners and spices), as many home kitchen scales don't accurately measure miniscule gram weights. In certain cases, when the weight measurement is not critical to success and it is more practical to measure in volume, weights have been omitted.

KNOW YOUR SALT

Salt is one of the most underrated ingredients in baking. It's necessary for balancing the sweetness of many desserts and brightening the overall flavor. Personally, I use three types of salt in baking and cooking: kosher salt, fine sea salt, and a coarse flaky salt for sprinkling on top.

All the volume measurements for salt in this book are based on coarse kosher salt. I use Diamond Crystal kosher salt, which has a coarser grain compared to other brands of kosher salt. If substituting another brand, use two-thirds as much by volume; and if substituting fine sea salt or table salt, use half as much by volume. For clarity, all recipes with more than a teaspoon of salt include a weight measurement. I do recommend weighing salt in bread and yeasted pastry recipes, where salt not only adds flavor but contributes to the strength of the dough and the rate at which it rises. Weight measurements are the same no matter what type of salt you use.

THINK OF TEMPERATURE AS AN INGREDIENT

The temperature of your ingredients plays a critical part in the success of a recipe. Pie crusts, for example, rely on cold ingredients to preserve their tender and flaky texture. If the dough gets too warm, the butter will melt before rather than during baking, resulting in a greasy, slumped crust. Cakes, on the other hand, usually call for room-temperature butter, eggs, and dairy to properly combine into a smooth, well-mixed batter. If the ingredients are too cold, you'll likely end up mixing too long and can end up with a tough and gummy cake. Give your ingredients enough time to get to the proper temperature for the best success.

The temperature of your oven is also important to monitor, as many ovens don't run true to dial. Investing in an oven thermometer can help you determine whether your oven runs hot or cold so you can adjust accordingly. Be sure to also preheat your oven thoroughly before baking.

USE PHYSICAL INDICATORS, NOT JUST TIME, TO DETERMINE DONENESS

One of the challenges of recipe writing is that there are many variables out of our control. We try to include a variety of useful information to help you succeed, but ultimately we don't know what kind of mixing equipment you have, the temperature of your kitchen, the materials of your bakeware—all things that can greatly affect how long it takes to finish a specific task or how long your batch of brownies will take to bake. Times can be used as guidelines, but the physical indicators—such as "knead until **smooth**," "let rise until **doubled**," "bake until **golden brown**"—are much more important. Pay attention throughout the baking process, training all your senses to understand when each step is finished before moving on to the next.

SUBSTITUTE THOUGHTFULLY

I'm a big fan of riffing on recipes and coming up with new variations on old favorites—that's why I wrote this book! However, I always recommend following a recipe as closely as possible the first time you try it. It's hard to know the effect of any substitutions and changes without first having a baseline for comparison. Once you know how a certain recipe is supposed to look and taste, then I encourage you to start making it your own. Limit yourself to one significant change each time so that you can really understand the impact it has on the final product, and write down the results for future reference. Not all your "bakexperiments" might work, so save the riskier ones for low-stakes occasions. But trying new ideas is how you will become a more confident and creative baker.

HAVE FUN!

Ultimately, baking should be fun. It's about celebrating the big and small moments in life and making something delicious for your friends and family. I hope these recipes will inspire you to express your creativity in the kitchen and put smiles on the faces of the people around you.

CAFÉ FAVORITES: QUICK BREADS *and* CAKES

For close to a year, I worked the opening shift at our local coffee shop. One of my favorite tasks was setting up the pastry case with muffins, scones, and loaf cakes in anticipation of the early rush. For many of our customers, these tasty treats were as much a part of their daily ritual as their morning latte.

These café-style baked goods—or quick breads, as they're often categorized—are an essential part of any home baker's repertoire. I like to think of the recipes in this chapter as "anytime" bakes that are easy to whip up whenever the urge to bake strikes and even easier to enjoy any time of the day. Quick breads aren't meant to be fancy; they're intended to be accessible, adaptable, and (as the name implies) quick to make.

But quick doesn't mean boring! On the contrary, these simple doughs and batters hold up well to tasty additions such as fruit, herbs, spices, nuts, and chocolate; and I've included some of my favorite variations for each recipe. Once you're familiar with the basic techniques for making flaky scones and tender cakes, go a step further and experiment with different spices and add-ins to put your personal signature on these recipes. Before you know it, your friends and family will be looking to you for that comforting slice of Not-Your-Grandma's Banana Bread (page 12) or a piping hot tray of Blueberry Streusel Muffins (page 16)—just have them bring the coffee!

NOT–YOUR–GRANDMA'S BANANA BREAD

MAKES ONE
9 X 4–INCH
(23 X 10–CM) OR
9 X 5–INCH
(23 X 13–CM) LOAF

400 g (1¾ cups) overripe bananas (about 3–4 medium bananas)

60 g (¼ cup) sour cream, at room temperature

110 g (½ cup) neutral vegetable oil, such as grapeseed or canola

150 g (¾ cup) light brown sugar

2 large eggs, at room temperature

1 tsp pure vanilla extract

250 g (2 cups) white whole-wheat flour or sifted whole-grain flour

1 tsp baking soda

½ tsp baking powder

¾ tsp kosher salt

1 tsp ground cinnamon

¼ tsp ground nutmeg

50 g (¼ cup) uncooked millet

85 g (½ cup) semi-sweet chocolate chips

30 g (2 tbsp) coarse sugar, for sprinkling

Every baker needs a solid banana bread recipe in their back pocket, and this is mine. It's morphed over the years from something that was much more like a banana cake—which has its place—into a still-delicious-but-a-little-healthier breakfast bread that is kid-approved. It's sneakily whole-grain and positively packed with bananas. We like ours with millet for crunch and chocolate for . . . well, chocolate, but you can easily swap out the add-ins to make this your own. I particularly like baking this loaf in a 9 x 4-inch (23 x 10-cm) Pullman pan for nice straight edges, but a 9 x 5-inch (23 x 13-cm) loaf pan works just as well.

Preheat the oven to 350°F (175°C) with a rack in the center. Line a 9 x 4-inch (23 x 10-cm) Pullman pan or loaf pan with a parchment paper sling, leaving about 3 inches (7.5 cm) of overhang on the long sides for easy removal. Lightly grease the pan and parchment.

Place the bananas in a large bowl and mash them with a wooden spoon or fork until mostly smooth; a few lumps are okay. Mix in the sour cream, oil, sugar, eggs, and vanilla until smooth.

In a medium bowl, whisk the flour, baking soda, baking powder, salt, cinnamon, and nutmeg together. Pour the dry ingredients into the wet and use a flexible spatula or wooden spoon to combine gently. When the batter is almost completely combined (there should still be a few streaks of flour visible), add the millet and chocolate chips. Mix until just combined.

Pour the batter into the prepared pan and level the top with a palette knife. Sprinkle with the coarse sugar.

Bake until the bread feels set on the top and a skewer inserted into the center comes out clean, or with just a few moist crumbs (but no wet batter), about 60 to 75 minutes. If the bread appears to be browning too quickly, tent it with foil for the final 15 to 20 minutes of baking.

Remove the bread from the oven. Cool in the pan for 15 minutes, then remove from the pan and cool completely on a wire rack. Store leftover bread, tightly wrapped, at room temperature for up to 5 days.

VARIATIONS

Banana Nut: Omit the millet and chocolate chips and mix in about 120 grams (1 cup) of toasted, chopped nuts (walnuts or pecans are particularly nice) after the flour.

Banana Pumpkin: Omit the sour cream. Reduce the banana to 230 grams (1 cup) and add 245 grams (1 cup) of pumpkin puree to the wet ingredients. For a more spice-forward loaf, replace the cinnamon and nutmeg with 7 grams (1 tbsp) of pumpkin pie spice.

Peanut Butter–Chocolate: Omit the sour cream and reduce the oil to 55 grams (¼ cup). Add 125 grams (½ cup) of well-stirred smooth peanut butter to the wet ingredients. Omit the millet and add 75 grams (½ cup) of chopped roasted peanuts in with the chocolate chips. After pouring the batter into the pan, dollop about 48 grams (3 tbsp) of peanut butter on top and use a knife to swirl it in.

Double Chocolate: Reduce the flour to 188 grams (1½ cups). Sift in 60 grams (½ cup) of Dutch-processed cocoa powder with the dry ingredients. Omit the millet and increase the chocolate chips to 170 grams (1 cup).

Muffins: This loaf can also be baked into muffins, for a yield of about 14 to 16 muffins. Fill muffin liners nearly to the top and bake at 375°F (190°C) for about 20 to 30 minutes.

LEMONIEST LEMON POPPYSEED LOAF

MAKES ONE
8½ X 4½-INCH
(22 X 11-CM) LOAF

LEMON POPPYSEED LOAF
150 g (¾ cup) granulated sugar
4 g (1 tbsp) lemon zest (from about 2 lemons)
192 g (1½ cups) flour, sifted
6 g (1½ tsp) baking powder
½ tsp kosher salt
3 large eggs, at room temperature
110 g (½ cup) neutral vegetable oil, such as grapeseed or canola
½ tsp lemon oil
1 tsp pure vanilla extract
120 g (½ cup) plain full-fat Greek yogurt, at room temperature
36 g (2½ tbsp) freshly squeezed lemon juice
27 g (3 tbsp) poppyseeds

LEMON SOAK
36 g (2½ tbsp) freshly squeezed lemon juice
38 g (3 tbsp) granulated sugar

This simple loaf cake packs a big citrusy punch thanks to lemon zest, lemon oil, and lemon juice in the batter. To add an extra layer of flavor, I like brushing a lemon soak onto the loaf right after it comes out of the oven. The loaf stays beautifully moist for days, and I often find myself sneaking slivers throughout the week for a quick treat.

Preheat the oven to 350°F (175°C) with a rack in the middle. Line an 8½ x 4½-inch (22 x 11-cm) loaf pan with parchment paper, leaving about 3 inches (7.5 cm) of overhang on the long sides for easy removal. Lightly grease the pan and parchment.

Make the Lemon Poppyseed Loaf: In the bowl of a stand mixer fitted with the whisk attachment, combine the sugar and the lemon zest. Rub the zest into the sugar until fragrant and damp to release the essential oils from the rind, which will intensify the lemon flavor.

In a small bowl, whisk together the flour, baking powder, and salt. Set aside.

Add the eggs to the sugar-zest mixture. Mix on low to combine, then increase the speed to medium-high and whip until the mixture is slightly thickened and lighter in color, about 2 minutes. (You can also make this using a handheld mixer or a whisk; it will just take a little longer.) Slowly stream in the vegetable oil, lemon oil, and vanilla. Continue mixing until well combined, about another 2 minutes.

Turn the mixer down to low and add half of the flour mixture, followed by the yogurt. Add the remaining flour mixture, then the lemon juice. Finally, add the poppyseeds, mixing just to combine. Use a flexible spatula to fold from the bottom of the bowl to make sure everything is well mixed and there are no pockets of unincorporated flour. Scrape the batter into the prepared pan and smooth the top.

Bake until the cake is golden brown and a skewer inserted in the center comes out clean or with a few moist crumbs, about 50 to 60 minutes.

Make the Lemon Soak: While the cake is baking, combine the lemon juice and sugar in a small saucepan. Cook over medium heat, stirring occasionally, until the sugar is dissolved. Remove from the heat and pour into a heatproof container.

To Finish: When the cake is done, transfer the pan to a wire rack. Use a skewer to poke holes all over the top and brush generously with about half of the lemon soak. Wait about 5 minutes for the liquid to absorb, then brush on more soak, using as much as possible. Allow the cake to cool in the pan for 10 to 15 minutes, then remove from the pan. Brush any remaining syrup on the sides of the cake. Allow the cake to cool completely before serving. For the best flavor, wrap the cooled cake in plastic wrap and let sit overnight to let the syrup fully soak in. Store the cake at room temperature, tightly wrapped, for up to 5 days.

VARIATIONS

Choose Your Own Citrus: Swap out the lemon juice and zest for another citrus fruit such as orange, lime, or grapefruit. The lemon oil can be replaced by a corresponding citrus oil or simply omitted.

Glaze It Up: Whisk together 60 grams (½ cup) of sifted icing sugar, 10 grams (2 tsp) of milk, 10 grams (2 tsp) of freshly squeezed lemon juice, and a pinch of salt to form a smooth, pourable glaze. Add more milk or lemon juice, if necessary, to achieve desired consistency. Pour or drizzle over the cooled (and soaked) cake. Garnish with a few gratings of the lemon zest, if desired. Let the glaze set for at least 10 minutes before serving.

Lemon-Lavender: For an added floral note, whisk 2½ tsp of culinary dried lavender in with the

BLUEBERRY STREUSEL MUFFINS

MAKES 12 MUFFINS

STREUSEL TOPPING

30 g (¼ cup) whole-wheat flour

30 g (2 tbsp) coarse sugar (such as demerara)

Pinch of salt

28 g (2 tbsp) unsalted butter, cold and cubed

BLUEBERRY MUFFINS

113 g (½ cup) unsalted butter, melted and cooled

65 g (⅓ cup) granulated sugar

65 g (⅓ cup) light brown sugar

2 large eggs, at room temperature

1 tsp pure vanilla extract

¼ tsp pure almond extract

160 g (⅔ cup) buttermilk, at room temperature

188 g (1½ cups) all-purpose flour

63 g (½ cup) whole-wheat flour

½ tsp kosher salt

8 g (2 tsp) baking powder

¼ tsp baking soda

10 g (2½ tbsp) lemon zest (from about 1 lemon)

3 g (1½ tsp) ground ginger

¼ tsp ground nutmeg

250 g (1½ cups) rinsed and dried blueberries, fresh or frozen (if frozen, do not defrost, see Baker's Notes)

Packed with plump blueberries, these tender muffins are a perennial breakfast favorite in our house. Ground ginger, lemon zest, and a touch of almond extract may not be your usual suspects in a blueberry muffin recipe, but I find they brighten and round out the flavor beautifully. A generous sprinkling of streusel adds some bakery-style pizzazz.

Preheat the oven to 425°F (220°C) with a rack in the middle. Line a standard 12-cup muffin tin with paper liners and lightly grease the liners. Grease the areas of the pan between the cups as well to ease removal of the muffins.

Make the Streusel Topping: In a small bowl, combine the flour, sugar, and salt. Scatter the cubed butter over the top and work it in with your fingertips until the mixture is sandy and crumbly. Refrigerate until needed.

Make the Blueberry Muffins: In a large bowl, whisk together the melted butter and sugars until smooth. Add the eggs, vanilla and almond extracts, and buttermilk and whisk to combine.

In a separate bowl, whisk together the flours, salt, baking powder, baking soda, lemon zest, ginger, and nutmeg until well combined.

Add the dry ingredients to the wet ingredients and fold together gently with a flexible spatula. When just a few streaks of flour remain, fold in the blueberries, being careful not to crush them. The batter will be very thick.

Divide the batter evenly among the muffin cups. They should be quite full. Sprinkle each muffin with streusel topping, squeezing the mixture together with your fingers to form larger clumps as desired. Gently press the streusel topping to adhere.

Bake at 425°F (220°C) for 5 minutes, then lower the temperature to 375°F (190°C) and bake for another 15 to 20 minutes, or until golden and springy to the touch. A skewer inserted into the center of a muffin should be clean of raw batter (there may be some blueberry juice).

Cool in the pan for 10 minutes, then remove and cool completely on a wire rack.

Leftover muffins can be stored in an airtight container for up to 2 days.

VARIATIONS

Loaf Cake: These muffins can also be baked as a single loaf cake. Scrape the batter into a parchment-lined 9 x 5—inch (23 x 13—cm) loaf pan, sprinkle streusel on top, and bake in a preheated 350°F (175°C) oven for about 45 to 60 minutes. Cool in the pan for 10 minutes, then turn out onto a wire rack to finish cooling completely.

Berry-Lime: Replace the lemon zest with lime zest and the blueberries with raspberries or blackberries (chopped if large).

Cherry-Almond: Replace the blueberries with 200 grams (1 cup) of pitted and chopped fresh sweet cherries and 70 grams (½ cup) of toasted, chopped almonds. Omit the vanilla and increase the almond extract to ¾ teaspoon.

BAKER'S NOTES

While I prefer using fresh blueberries when available, frozen berries work well, too. Don't defrost them before adding to the batter. Muffins using frozen berries will likely take at least 5 minutes longer to bake as the frozen berries cool down the batter considerably. The finished muffins may have tinges of green from where the berries bleed into the batter, but they will still taste wonderful.

If you don't want to make the streusel topping, you can sprinkle the top of each muffin with 1 teaspoon of coarse sugar for added sweetness and crunch.

BROWN BUTTER MINI MUFFIN FINANCIERS

**MAKES ABOUT
15 FINANCIERS**

Softened unsalted butter, for greasing the pan
113 g (½ cup) unsalted butter, cubed
120 g (1 cup) icing sugar, sifted
100 g (1 cup) almond flour
25 g (3 tbsp) all-purpose flour
¼ tsp fine sea salt
120 g (½ cup) egg whites (from about 4 large eggs), at room temperature
½ tsp pure vanilla extract
Icing sugar, for garnishing (optional)

These dense little cakes are packed with flavor thanks to the duo of ground almonds and brown butter. They're my favorite thing to make whenever I have a few spare egg whites. Financiers are traditionally baked in special rectangular molds. The finished cakes resemble gold bars, hence the name. But since most people I know—including myself—don't own these special molds, a mini muffin tin makes a perfect substitute.

Preheat the oven to 400°F (200°C) with a rack in the middle, and grease the cups of a mini muffin tin with softened butter.

To brown the butter, place the cubed butter in a small, light-colored saucepan over low-medium heat. Once the butter has melted, turn the heat up to medium-high. Stir frequently with a heatproof spatula, scraping the sides and bottom of the pan as needed. The butter will crackle, foam, turn clear gold, then finally start browning. It's done when the crackling subsides and you smell toasted nuts. This process takes about 10 minutes total, but the butter can go from browned to burnt in a flash—so keep an eye on it.

Pour the butter and all the toasty bits into a small bowl or glass measuring cup and allow to cool slightly (it should be warm but not piping hot when you add it to the rest of the ingredients).

In a separate bowl, whisk together the icing sugar, flours, and salt.

Whisk the egg whites just to loosen them. Make a well in the center of the dry ingredients and pour in the egg whites and vanilla. Whisk to combine.

Add the browned butter to the batter and whisk until the butter is completely incorporated. Cover and refrigerate for at least 2 hours, or up to 3 days, to meld the flavors and make the batter easier to portion.

Divide the batter evenly between the cups of the muffin pan, filling each cup almost to the top. Tap the pan on the counter a couple of times to level the batter.

Bake for 12 to 15 minutes, or until the centers are puffed and set and the edges are golden brown.

Cool the financiers in the tin for 2 to 3 minutes, then carefully turn them out and allow to cool completely on a wire rack. Dust with icing sugar before serving, if desired.

Store leftovers in an airtight container for up to 5 days.

VARIATIONS

Berry: Press a blueberry, raspberry, or blackberry (halved if large) into the center of each financier before baking.

Black Sesame: Decrease the almond flour to 50 grams (½ cup). In a small skillet, toast 50 grams (5½ tbsp) of black sesame seeds until fragrant. Cool completely, then grind into a powder in a spice or coffee grinder. Whisk black sesame powder in with dry ingredients.

Other Nut Flours: Substitute some, or all, of the almond flour with another type of nut flour or finely ground nuts, such as pecans, hazelnuts, pistachios, or walnuts.

Coffee or Tea: Whisk in 3 grams (2 tsp) of culinary-grade matcha or espresso powder with the dry ingredients.

SPICED COFFEE CRUMB CAKE

MAKES ONE 9–INCH (23–CM) CAKE

A tender spice-kissed cake topped with a layer of buttery crumbs is my idea of the perfect anytime cake. A moderate dose of sour cream in the batter keeps this coffee cake moist for days, if it lasts that long.

STREUSEL MIXTURE
63 g (½ cup) whole-wheat flour
65 g (⅓ cup) light brown sugar
1 tsp ground cinnamon
¼ tsp kosher salt
56 g (4 tbsp) unsalted butter, cold and cut into ¼-inch (6-mm) cubes

SPICED CAKE
113 g (½ cup) unsalted butter, at room temperature
150 g (¾ cup) granulated sugar
½ tsp kosher salt
5 g (1¼ tsp) baking powder
¼ tsp baking soda
½ tsp ground cinnamon
½ tsp ground ginger
¼ tsp ground cardamom
¼ tsp ground nutmeg
⅛ tsp allspice
2 large eggs, at room temperature
10 g (2 tsp) pure vanilla extract
188 g (1½ cups) all-purpose flour
160 g (⅔ cup) sour cream or full-fat plain Greek yogurt, at room temperature

SOUR CREAM GLAZE
120 g (1 cup) icing sugar
30 g (2 tbsp) sour cream
Pinch of salt
Milk or water, as needed

Preheat the oven to 350°F (175°C) with a rack in the middle. Lightly grease a 9-inch (23-cm) springform or loose-bottomed cake pan and line the bottom with parchment paper. Lightly grease and flour the pan and parchment.

Make the Streusel Mixture: In a medium bowl, whisk together the flour, sugar, cinnamon, and salt. Scatter the butter pieces over the top. Use your fingers to rub the butter into the dry ingredients until the mixture resembles damp sand, with no dry bits remaining. Refrigerate until needed.

Make the Spiced Cake Batter: In the bowl of a stand mixer fitted with the paddle attachment, combine the butter, sugar, salt, baking powder, baking soda, cinnamon, ginger, cardamom, nutmeg, and allspice. Mix on low to combine, then increase the speed to medium and cream until light and fluffy, about 4 to 5 minutes. Scrape down the sides of the bowl and the paddle a couple times during this process to ensure even mixing.

Add the eggs one at a time, mixing well after each. Add the vanilla. Mix well to combine. Scrape down the bowl and paddle.

With the mixer running on low, add the flour and sour cream in five additions, beginning and ending with the flour. Use a flexible spatula to fold from the bottom of the bowl a few times to make sure the batter is well mixed.

Scrape half of the cake batter into the prepared pan. Use a small offset spatula to smooth it into an even layer. Sprinkle half of the streusel mixture evenly over the top. Dollop the remaining cake batter on top and gently smooth into an even layer. Sprinkle the remaining streusel mixture evenly over the top, squeezing handfuls together to create some larger clumps of topping.

Bake until the cake is puffed and the top is evenly golden and a skewer inserted into the center of the cake comes out clean or with a few moist crumbs, about 40 to 50 minutes. Cool in the pan for 10 minutes, then remove and finish cooling completely on a wire rack before glazing.

Make the Sour Cream Glaze: Sift the icing sugar into a small bowl. Add the sour cream and salt and whisk thoroughly to combine. Add milk or water 1 teaspoon at a time, whisking well after each addition, until desired glaze consistency is reached. Use immediately, spooning or drizzling the glaze over the cake as desired. Allow the glaze to set for about 10 minutes before serving. Store leftovers in an airtight container at room temperature for up to 5 days.

VARIATIONS

Nut Streusel: Add up to 60 grams (½ cup) of chopped or sliced nuts to the streusel, mixing them in after the butter.

Berry-Almond: Add 60 grams (½ cup) of sliced almonds to the streusel. Replace the ground spices with the zest of 1 lemon and add ½ teaspoon of pure almond extract with the vanilla. Gently fold about 150 grams (1 cup) of fresh blueberries, raspberries, or blackberries into the cake batter after all the flour has been added. For added brightness, substitute lemon juice for the sour cream in the glaze. For this variation, I like to sprinkle all the streusel mixture on top of the cake.

Apple-Rye: Replace the whole-wheat flour in the streusel with rye flour. Use 125 grams (1 cup) of all-purpose flour and 63 grams (⅔ cup) of rye flour in the cake batter. Peel and dice 1 medium-to-large baking apple and sprinkle with a squeeze of lemon juice. Gently fold diced apple into the cake batter after all the flour has been added. For this variation, I like to sprinkle all the streusel mixture on top of the cake.

Coffee-Cardamom: Add 1 teaspoon of espresso powder and ¼ teaspoon of ground cardamom to the streusel. Omit the ground ginger and allspice and add 6 grams (1 tbsp) of espresso powder to the cake batter with the spices. Substitute strongly brewed coffee or espresso for the sour cream in the glaze.

BAKER'S NOTES

This cake can also be baked in a parchment-lined 9 x 9–inch (23 x 23–cm) pan with at least 2-inch (5-cm) sides. It will bake slightly quicker; start checking for doneness around 35 minutes.

RASPBERRY–WHITE CHOCOLATE SCONES

250 g (2 cups) all-purpose flour

63 g (½ cup) whole-wheat flour (or substitute more all-purpose flour)

50 g (¼ cup) granulated sugar

12 g (1 tbsp) baking powder

¾ tsp kosher salt

85 g (6 tbsp) unsalted butter, cold and cut into ½-inch (1.25-cm) cubes

120 g (½ cup) cold heavy cream, plus more for brushing on tops of scones

60 g (¼ cup) sour cream, cold

1 large egg, cold

8 g (1½ tsp) pure vanilla extract

100 g (¾ cup) fresh or frozen raspberries (if frozen, do not defrost)

70 g (½ cup) white chocolate, chopped

Coarse sugar, for sprinkling

My ideal scone is crisp on the outside and tender on the inside with just enough mix-ins to keep each bite interesting. The keys to a good rise and texture are keeping your ingredients cold and gently handling the dough. I love the tart-sweet combination of fresh raspberries and white chocolate, but see the variations on the next page for a few more of my favorite flavor combos.

Preheat the oven to 425°F (220°C) with a rack in the middle. Stack two baking sheets together and line the top one with parchment paper. (This keeps the bottoms from scorching during baking.)

In a medium bowl, whisk together the flours, sugar, baking powder, and salt. Add the cold, cubed butter to the dry ingredients and cut it in using a pastry cutter or your fingers. You should have butter pieces ranging in size from peas to walnuts.

In a separate bowl, whisk together the heavy cream, sour cream, egg, and vanilla. Pour over the dry ingredients and gently fold in with a spatula until combined. The dough should be a bit shaggy but should hold together. If not, add more cold cream 1 teaspoon at a time until it does.

Tip the dough onto a lightly floured surface and knead a few times to bring it together. Roll the dough into a 12-inch (30-cm) square, flouring the dough and pin just enough to avoid sticking. Brush off any excess flour. Fold the dough in thirds like a letter, rotate 90 degrees, then fold in thirds again so you have a 4-inch (10-cm) square. Transfer to a baking sheet and freeze for 10 minutes.

After chilling, return the dough to your lightly floured surface. Roll it again into a 12-inch (30-cm) square. Sprinkle the raspberries and white chocolate evenly over the dough, then roll it up like a jelly roll. Turn the dough so the seam side is down, then gently pat it into a 12 x 4–inch (30 x 10–cm) rectangle. If the dough feels soft or sticky at all, freeze for 5 to 10 minutes to make it easier to cut. Using a sharp knife, cut the dough into four equal pieces, then cut each piece on the diagonal to create 8 triangular scones. Cut straight down to preserve the layers and help the scones rise evenly in the oven. Transfer the scones to the prepared baking sheet and freeze while the oven finishes preheating.

When the oven is ready, brush the tops of the scones gently with cream and sprinkle generously with coarse sugar. Bake for 20 to 30 minutes, rotating halfway through, until the tops and bottoms are golden brown. Cool on a wire rack for 10 minutes before serving. Scones are best freshly baked, but you can store them well wrapped at room temperature for a few days. Reheat for 5 to 10 minutes in a 350°F (175°C) oven. You can also freeze unbaked scones and bake them straight from frozen (you may need an extra 2 to 3 minutes of baking time).

VARIATIONS

Scones are a wonderful vehicle for in-season fruit, and you can replace the raspberries and white chocolate in this recipe with about 1 cup dried, fresh, or frozen fruit. However, if your fruits are extremely juicy (think peak season fresh peaches and strawberries), dice and drain them in a sieve to remove some of the extra liquid before adding them to your dough.

Lemon-Blueberry: Add the zest of 1 lemon to the dry ingredients and ½ teaspoon of pure almond extract to the wet ingredients. Replace the white chocolate and raspberries with about 150 grams (1 cup) of fresh blueberries.

Cranberry, Orange, and Pecan: Add the zest of 1 orange to the dry ingredients. Replace the white chocolate and raspberries with about 60 grams (½ cup) of dried cranberries and 55 grams (½ cup) of toasted, chopped pecans.

Dark Chocolate–Cherry: Add ½ teaspoon of pure almond extract to the wet ingredients. Replace the white chocolate and raspberries with about 90 grams (¾ cup) of dried cherries and 45 grams (¼ cup) of chopped dark chocolate.

Cheddar-Scallion: Reduce sugar to 12 grams (1 tbsp) and salt to ½ teaspoon. Replace the white chocolate and raspberries with about 100 grams (1 cup) of shredded sharp cheddar cheese and 3 finely chopped scallions; sprinkle tops of scones with a little more grated cheese before baking.

Gingerbread: Add 1 teaspoon of ground ginger, 1 teaspoon of ground cinnamon, ½ teaspoon of ground cardamom, and ¼ teaspoon each of ground nutmeg, allspice, and cloves to the dry ingredients. Replace the white chocolate and raspberries with about 60 grams (½ cup) of dried currants or cranberries and 90 grams (½ cup) of chopped crystallized ginger.

BAKER'S NOTES

The rolling and folding technique for these scones comes from America's Test Kitchen. It helps create an extra flaky scone by mimicking how layers are added in laminated doughs such as puff pastry.

If you prefer less flaky, more cake-like scones, add your mix-ins to the dry ingredients before combining with the wet ingredients. Once the dough comes together, form into a 6-inch (15-cm) round and cut into 8 wedges. Freeze while the oven preheats and bake as directed.

FLAKY BUTTERMILK BISCUITS, INFINITELY RIFFABLE

MAKES 8 SQUARE BISCUITS

280 g (2¼ cups) all-purpose flour

5 g (1¼ tsp) kosher salt

10 g (2 tsp) granulated sugar

8 g (2 tsp) baking powder

¼ tsp baking soda

113 g (½ cup) unsalted butter, cold and cut into ½-inch (1.25-cm) cubes

180 g (¾ cup) cold buttermilk, plus more as needed

Melted butter or milk, for brushing (optional)

Whether slathered with jam or dunked into soup, biscuits add a warm and comforting touch to any meal of the day. Like pie dough and scones, biscuits depend on cold ingredients and a gentle touch to rise flaky and tender. This basic recipe makes a lovely plain biscuit that can accommodate a cup or so of mix-ins, so dress them up however you like—sweet or savory. I like the simplicity of cutting biscuits with a sharp knife or bench scraper, but you can use a round biscuit cutter as well. Flour the cutter and press straight down when cutting the biscuits, as twisting can warp the layers and create uneven biscuits.

Preheat the oven to 425°F (220°C) with a rack in the center.

In a large bowl, whisk together the flour, salt, sugar, baking powder, and baking soda. Scatter the cold butter pieces over the top and, using your fingers or a pastry blender, cut it into the flour mixture until the butter pieces are roughly the size of peas.

Drizzle the buttermilk over the top and gently fold it into the flour mixture using a fork or flexible spatula. Continue to fold the dough onto itself a few times, just until the dough holds together but is still a bit shaggy with a few dry spots. If the dough seems overly dry and won't come together, drizzle in extra buttermilk 1 teaspoon at a time, just until it forms a rough mass. Do not overwork the dough.

Turn the dough onto a piece of parchment paper and fold it gently a few times until cohesive. Use your hands to pat it into a rectangle about 1 inch (2.5 cm) thick. Using a bench scraper or sharp knife, cut the dough into quarters. Stack the pieces on top of each other, sandwiching any stray floury bits between the layers, then pat or gently roll into a rectangle about 4 x 8 inches (10 x 20 cm). (If you want, trim a thin strip off each side of the rectangle—this will help the biscuits rise more evenly. But to be honest, I rarely bother.) Slide the dough still on the parchment onto a sheet tray and freeze for 15 minutes or until chilled, but not completely hard.

When ready to bake, cut the chilled dough into eight 2-inch (5-cm) squares. You can keep the biscuits on the sheet tray or, for crispier bottoms, transfer to a cast-iron pan that is at least 8 inches (20 cm). Either way, arrange them closely together for the highest rise. Brush the tops with melted butter or milk, if desired. Bake for 20 to 25 minutes, or until the edges and tops are golden. Cool on the pan for 5 minutes before serving.

VARIATIONS

Feel free to be creative with your mix-ins, avoiding any ingredients that are too wet (such as very juicy fruits or purees), which will throw the liquids out of balance. Keep the amount to about 1 to 1¼ cups so you don't overload the dough and make it difficult for the biscuits to rise.

Cheddar-Chive: Add 100 grams (1 cup) of shredded sharp cheddar cheese and 20 grams (¼ cup) of finely chopped chives to the flour-butter mixture before adding the buttermilk. Sprinkle the tops of the biscuits with a little extra cheddar before baking.

Everything Bagel: Before baking, brush the biscuits with melted butter and sprinkle with everything bagel spice blend: 2 teaspoons of white sesame seeds, 1½ teaspoons each of dried minced garlic, dried minced onion, and black sesame seeds, 1 teaspoon of flaky sea salt, and ½ teaspoon of poppy seeds. Serve with softened cream cheese.

Shortcake: Before baking, brush the biscuits with melted butter and sprinkle with coarse sugar. Split cooled biscuits in half and top with freshly whipped cream and lightly sweetened berries.

Rich Biscuits: For richer biscuits, substitute some, or all, of the buttermilk with an equal amount of heavy cream or sour cream. I particularly like using half buttermilk and half sour cream.

ANYTIME TREATS: COOKIES *and* BARS

It's always the right time for a cookie, whether it's a crisp Chocolate-Almond Biscotti (page 46) to accompany a morning coffee, a chewy oatmeal raisin cookie to satisfy a midafternoon craving, or the fudgy My Best Brownies (page 34) to end a meal.

While you can't go wrong with classic flavors, cookies and bars are also incredibly easy to customize. Start by simply swapping out the add-ins, or try substituting a small percentage of flour for a flavorful whole-grain variety. Jazz up shortbread cookies with a drizzle of chocolate, or make a variety of flavored sugars for our Choose-Your-Own-Adventure Snickerdoodles (page 32) extravaganza.

Making a batch of cookies or bars is also one of the best ways to share the joy of baking both inside and outside of the kitchen. Drop cookies are perfect for baking with kids—my little ones love measuring and pouring in the mix-ins for the Spelt and Honey Oatmeal Raisin Cookies (page 30) and rolling snickerdoodle dough in sugar. The recipes in this chapter also package and travel well, making them my go-tos for potlucks, care packages, and bake sales. Don't be shy about sharing your creations—it's a surefire way to sweeten someone's day!

SALTED BROWN BUTTER CHOCOLATE CHUNK COOKIES

MAKES 12–14 COOKIES

113 g (½ cup) unsalted butter, cubed

100 g (½ cup) light brown sugar

65 g (⅓ cup) granulated sugar

1 large egg, cold

1 large egg yolk, cold

8 g (1½ tsp) pure vanilla extract

62 g (½ cup) bread flour

62 g (½ cup) all-purpose flour

50 g (½ cup) rye flour

½ tsp baking powder

½ tsp baking soda

¾ tsp kosher salt

4 g (1 tbsp) finely ground coffee or 1 tsp espresso powder

140 g (¾ cup plus 1 tbsp) good-quality chopped dark chocolate

Flaky salt, for garnishing

Finding the perfect chocolate chip cookie recipe is the holy grail for many home bakers. I have several chocolate chip cookie recipes that I love, each being perfect for different reasons or occasions. But if I had to choose just one to keep in my arsenal, this would be it. This recipe uses a few tricks to produce a cookie packed with flavor and texture. Brown butter, brown sugar, and an extra yolk help create rich, fudgy centers. Bread flour keeps the cookies thick while rye flour adds complexity. A dose of coffee and salt tame the sweetness. Chilling the dough helps the flours better absorb all the liquid and gives the cookies deeper, more caramel-like flavor. Finally, using good-quality chopped chocolate as opposed to chips creates irregular pockets of melted chocolate throughout each bite. A little fussy for a cookie? Maybe, but I hope you'll try this recipe at least once, take a bite, and agree with me that yes—it's perfect.

To brown the butter, place it in a small, light-colored saucepan over low-medium heat. Once the butter has melted, turn the heat up to medium-high. Stir frequently with a heatproof spatula, scraping the sides and bottom of the pan as needed. The butter will crackle, foam, turn clear gold, then finally start browning. It's done when the crackling subsides and you smell toasted nuts. This process takes about 10 minutes total, but the butter can go from browned to burnt in a flash—so keep an eye on it. Scrape the butter and all the toasty bits into a large bowl and let cool for 5 minutes.

Whisk the sugars into the butter until smooth and combined, followed by the egg and egg yolk. Whisk in the vanilla. In a separate bowl, whisk together the flours, baking powder, baking soda, salt, and coffee. Add the dry ingredients to the wet and fold together until just combined. When just a few streaks of flour remain, add the chocolate, and mix until evenly distributed.

Portion the dough into ping-pong-sized balls, about 50 grams (3 tbsp) each, and place them on a parchment-lined baking sheet. (If the dough is too soft, cover and chill for about 30 minutes before scooping.) Cover and chill at least 4 hours, or up to 3 days.

When ready to bake, preheat the oven to 350°F (175°C) with a rack in the middle and line two baking sheets with parchment paper. Place the cookies on the prepared baking sheets about 2½ inches (6 cm) apart and sprinkle the tops with flaky sea salt.

Bake the cookies one sheet at a time until the edges are golden but the centers are still soft and just set, about 12 to 14 minutes. Rotate the sheet in the oven halfway through baking. Cool the cookies on the baking sheets for about 5 minutes, then transfer to a wire rack to cool completely. Store leftovers in an airtight container.

VARIATIONS

Whole-Grain Swap: An equal weight of another whole-grain flour can be substituted for the rye flour. I particularly like spelt or buckwheat in this recipe.

Double Chocolate–Walnut: Use 50 grams (⅓ cup plus 1 tbsp) each of bread and all-purpose flour and 50 grams (½ cup) of rye flour and add 30 grams (¼ cup) of Dutch-processed cocoa powder. Add 100 grams (1 cup) of toasted and chopped walnuts with the chocolate.

Triple Chocolate: Use 56 grams (⅓ cup) each of chopped dark, milk, and white chocolate.

Toffee: Add 50 grams (⅓ cup) of toffee bits with the chocolate.

Milk Chocolate–Hazelnut: Replace the dark chocolate with milk chocolate and mix in 60 grams (½ cup) of toasted and chopped hazelnuts with the chocolate.

Pretzel: Add 65 grams (1 cup) of chopped mini pretzels with the chocolate and top each cookie with a whole mini pretzel before baking.

BAKER'S NOTES

Unbaked cookie dough freezes well for up to 3 months. Freeze portioned dough on a baking sheet, then transfer to a large re-sealable bag for storage. Bake straight from the freezer. Frozen cookies may need to bake for about 2 to 3 extra minutes.

SPELT & HONEY OATMEAL RAISIN COOKIES

MAKES ABOUT
15 COOKIES

113 g (½ cup) unsalted butter, at room temperature

70 g (⅓ cup plus 1 tsp) light brown sugar

70 g (⅓ cup plus 1 tsp) granulated sugar

40 g (2 tbsp) honey

¾ tsp baking soda

¼ tsp baking powder

½ tsp ground cinnamon

¼ tsp ground ginger

¾ tsp kosher salt

1 large egg, at room temperature

8 g (1½ tsp) pure vanilla extract

125 g (1 cup) spelt flour

150 g (1⅔ cups) rolled oats (not quick)

90 g (⅔ cup) raisins

63 g (½ cup) toasted walnuts, chopped

Oatmeal raisin cookies are my idea of a perfect midafternoon treat, especially if they're thick and chewy with a hint of warm spices and a scattering of toasted nuts. Spelt flour adds an extra layer of nuttiness (and a hint of virtue). Honey is my secret weapon in these cookies—they help keep these cookies beautifully soft for days.

In the bowl of a stand mixer fitted with the paddle attachment, combine the butter, sugars, honey, baking soda, baking powder, cinnamon, ginger, and salt. Mix on low to combine, then increase the speed to medium and cream until light and fluffy, about 5 minutes. Scrape down the sides of the bowl and the paddle a couple of times during this process to ensure even mixing.

Reduce the mixer speed to low and add the egg and vanilla. Increase the speed to medium and mix until smooth. Scrape down the bowl and paddle.

With the mixer on low, add the flour. When there are just a few streaks of flour remaining, add the oats, followed by the raisins and walnuts. Mix just until combined. Use a flexible spatula to stir from the bottom of the bowl a few times to make sure everything is well mixed and there are no pockets of unincorporated flour. Cover and chill until just firm, about 45 minutes.

While the dough is chilling, preheat the oven to 350°F (175°C) with a rack in the middle and line two baking sheets with parchment paper.

Portion the dough into ping-pong-sized balls, about 50 grams (3 tbsp) each. Place the cookies on the prepared baking sheets about 2½ inches (6 cm) apart.

Bake the cookies one sheet at a time until the edges are golden but the centers are still soft and pale, about 13 to 15 minutes. Rotate the sheet in the oven halfway through baking. Cool the cookies on the baking sheets for about 5 minutes, then transfer to a wire rack to cool completely. Store leftovers in an airtight container.

VARIATIONS

Cranberry-Pistachio: Omit the raisins and walnuts. Add 90 grams (¾ cup) of dried cranberries and 50 grams (½ cup) of toasted, chopped pistachios.

Oatmeal–Chocolate Chunk: Omit the raisins and walnuts. Add 170 grams (1 cup) of chopped semi-sweet or bittersweet chocolate.

Monster Cookies: Omit the ground ginger, raisins, and walnuts. Add 125 grams (½ cup) of creamy peanut butter before adding the egg and vanilla. Add 100 grams (½ cup) of M&M'S® and 90 grams (½ cup) of chocolate chips after the oats.

Cookie Bars: Press the cookie dough (no need to chill) evenly into an 8 x 8-inch (20 x 20-cm) parchment-lined pan. Bake at 350°F (175°C) until edges are golden brown and middle is barely set, about 25 to 30 minutes. Cool completely in the pan before cutting into squares.

BAKER'S NOTES

Unbaked cookies freeze well for up to 3 months but tend not to spread as much because the oats absorb liquid. For best results, press the tops down lightly before freezing and bring to room temperature and bake as directed. To encourage spread, use a spatula to press down on the cookies halfway through baking.

CHOOSE–YOUR–OWN–ADVENTURE SNICKERDOODLES

Snickerdoodles are the comfy sweater of cookies, with their cozy cinnamon-sugar vibes and everyday appeal. I like using melted butter, bread flour, and a touch of brown sugar for cookies that bake up thick with extra-plush centers. In addition to enjoying the classic flavor, try customizing your snickerdoodles by switching up the sugar coating and amping up the spices in the dough.

MAKES ABOUT 24 COOKIES

227 g (1 cup) unsalted butter
188 g (1½ cups) bread flour
167 g (1⅓ cups) all-purpose flour
8 g (2 tsp) cream of tartar
1 tsp baking soda
1 tsp kosher salt
1 tsp ground cinnamon
200 g (1 cup) granulated sugar
65 g (⅓ cup) light brown sugar
2 large eggs, at room temperature
10 g (2 tsp) pure vanilla extract

SUGAR COATING
50 g (¼ cup) granulated sugar
8 g (1 tbsp) ground cinnamon

In a small saucepan over low heat, melt the butter. Transfer the melted butter to a large bowl and allow to cool slightly while you prepare the remaining ingredients.

In a small bowl, whisk together the flours, cream of tartar, baking soda, salt, and cinnamon. Set aside.

Whisk the sugars into the melted butter until smooth. Add the eggs and vanilla and whisk until incorporated. Add the dry ingredients and mix just until combined. Cover and refrigerate for about 30 to 60 minutes to allow the dough to hydrate and solidify slightly. (Cookie dough can be chilled for up to 5 days; if chilled for more than 2 hours, allow dough to soften for 20 to 30 minutes at room temperature for easier portioning.)

About 30 minutes before baking, preheat the oven to 375°F (190°C) with a rack in the center. Line two to three baking sheets with parchment paper.

Prepare the sugar coating by whisking together the granulated sugar and cinnamon.

Portion the cookie dough into golf-sized balls, about 40 grams (2 tbsp) each. Roll the dough between your hands into a smooth ball, then toss it in sugar coating. Place the cookies on the prepared baking sheets about 2 inches (5 cm) apart. Sprinkle each with a bit more sugar coating.

Bake sheets one at a time for 9 to 11 minutes, rotating the pan halfway through. The cookies should be puffed and the tops starting to crack, but the centers should still look a little soft. After removing the pan, bang it on the counter a couple of times to help deflate the cookies and get that classic crinkled top. Sprinkle with a bit more sugar coating. Cool cookies on the pan for about 5 minutes, then transfer to a wire rack to cool completely.

VARIATIONS

Gingerbread Latte: Omit the cinnamon from the dough. Make a gingerbread spice mix by combining 1½ teaspoons each of ground cinnamon and ground ginger, ¾ teaspoon of ground cardamom, ½ teaspoon of allspice, ¼ teaspoon each of ground nutmeg and ground cloves, and a few cracks of black pepper. Add 1½ teaspoons of the spice mix and 1 teaspoon of espresso powder to the dry ingredients. Use 50 grams (¼ cup) of light brown sugar, 1 teaspoon of espresso powder, and the remaining spice mix for the sugar coating.

Berry-Lemon: Omit the cinnamon from the dough. Add the zest of 1 lemon to the dough along with the sugars and replace 1 teaspoon of the vanilla with 1 teaspoon of lemon oil. Use 50 grams (¼ cup) of granulated sugar and 8 grams (2 tbsp) of finely ground freeze-dried strawberries, raspberries, or blueberries for the sugar coating.

Matcha: Omit the cinnamon from the dough. Add 2 teaspoons of culinary-grade matcha powder to the dry ingredients and reduce the vanilla to 1 teaspoon. Use 50 grams (¼ cup) of granulated sugar and 3 grams (2 tsp) of matcha powder for the sugar coating.

Spicy Chocolate: Reduce the bread flour to 125 grams (1 cup). Sift 60 grams (½ cup) of Dutch-processed cocoa powder and 1 teaspoon of espresso powder into the dry ingredients. Use 50 grams (¼ cup) of granulated sugar, 8 grams (1 tbsp) of cinnamon, ½ teaspoon of cayenne powder, and ¼ teaspoon each of smoked paprika and finely ground Szechuan peppercorns for the sugar coating. Before baking, use your palm or the bottom of a small glass to flatten the cookie dough into ½-inch (1.25-cm) thick discs (the added cocoa powder causes this version to spread less).

BAKER'S NOTES

Unbaked cookie dough freezes well for up to 3 months. Freeze the portioned dough on a baking sheet, then transfer to a large resealable bag for storage. Take the frozen cookie dough out of the freezer while preheating the oven, then toss in the sugar coating right before baking.

MY BEST BROWNIES

85 g (½ cup) bittersweet chocolate, chopped

85 g (6 tbsp) unsalted butter, cubed

75 g (⅓ cup) neutral vegetable oil, such as grapeseed or canola

94 g (¾ cup) all-purpose flour

60 g (½ cup) Dutch-processed cocoa powder, sifted

169 g (¾ cup plus 1 tbsp) granulated sugar

65 g (⅓ cup) light brown sugar

¾ tsp kosher salt

3 large eggs, cold

8 g (1½ tsp) pure vanilla extract

1 tsp espresso powder

Flaky sea salt, for sprinkling (optional)

As much as I like trying new recipes and flavors, the dessert I crave most often is a good old-fashioned brownie. My ideal brownie is rich and deeply chocolatey and crowned with a shiny, crackly top. This recipe checks all those boxes for me. I often bake batches to store in the freezer for a chocolate emergency—otherwise known as a Tuesday night after the kids have gone to sleep.

Preheat the oven to 350°F (175°C) with a rack in the middle. Line an 8 x 8-inch (20 x 20-cm) pan with foil or parchment, leaving about 3 inches (7.5 cm) of overhang on two sides, and lightly grease.

Place the chopped chocolate in a small glass measuring cup with a spout.

Place the butter in a small, light-colored saucepan over medium-low heat. Once the butter has melted, turn the heat up to medium-high. Stir frequently with a heatproof spatula, scraping the sides and bottom of the pan as needed. The butter will crackle, foam, turn clear gold, then finally start browning. It's done when the crackling subsides and you smell toasted nuts. This process takes about 10 minutes total, but the butter can go from browned to burnt in a flash—so keep an eye on it. Pour the butter and all the toasty bits over the chocolate. Add the oil and set aside.

In a small bowl, whisk together the flour and cocoa powder.

Combine the sugars, salt, eggs, vanilla, and espresso powder in the bowl of a stand mixer fitted with the whisk attachment (or use a handheld mixer). Whisk on low briefly to combine, then turn up the speed to medium-high and continue whisking until the mixture is thick, pale, and roughly tripled in size, about 5 to 6 minutes.

Reduce the speed to low and drizzle in the butter-chocolate-oil mixture. Once incorporated, add the flour-cocoa mixture, mixing just to combine. Use a flexible spatula to fold from the bottom of the bowl to make sure everything is well mixed and there are no pockets of unincorporated flour.

Pour the batter into the prepared pan and sprinkle generously with flaky sea salt, if desired. Bake until the top is cracked and glossy and a toothpick inserted in the middle comes out with just a few moist crumbs, about 25 to 30 minutes. Cool brownies completely in the pan on a wire rack before slicing. In an airtight container, brownies will keep at room temperature for up to 5 days or in the freezer for up to 3 months.

VARIATIONS

Rye: Replace half of the all-purpose flour with whole-grain rye flour, which intensifies the chocolatey flavor.

Peppermint Bark: Add ½ teaspoon of peppermint extract to the brownie batter. Fold in 85 grams (½ cup) of chopped peppermint bark after the flour and sprinkle the top with peppermint bark bits instead of flaky salt.

Cream Cheese Swirl: Before preparing the brownie batter, beat together 250 grams (1 block) of room-temperature cream cheese and 50 grams (¼ cup) of granulated sugar until smooth. Add 1 teaspoon of pure vanilla extract and 1 large room temperature egg and beat until smooth. Prepare the brownie batter as directed. Scrape the brownie batter into the prepared pan, reserving about ⅓ cup. Pour the cream cheese batter over the top. Dollop the reserved brownie batter on top. Use a knife or skewer to swirl the brownie batter and cream cheese batter together. Bake as directed.

Cherry-Walnut: Fold in 55 grams (½ cup) of chopped, fresh cherries and 55 grams (½ cup) of chopped, toasted walnuts after the flour.

BAKER'S NOTES

For clean brownie slices, chill the brownies in the fridge before slicing with a sharp chef's knife. Wipe the knife clean with a hot towel between slices.

ESPRESSO–HAZELNUT BLONDIES

**MAKES ONE
8 X 8–INCH
(20 X 20–CM) PAN**

70 g (½ cup) raw hazelnuts
150 g (¾ cup) light brown sugar
50 g (¼ cup) granulated sugar
¾ tsp kosher salt
113 g (½ cup) unsalted butter, cubed
1 large egg, cold
1 large egg yolk, cold
30 g (2 tbsp) freshly brewed espresso or strong coffee
1 tsp espresso powder
10 g (2 tsp) pure vanilla extract
125 g (1 cup) all-purpose flour, sifted
Flaky salt, for garnishing (optional)

For a long time, I didn't understand the appeal of blondies, writing them off as inferior brownies. Then one day I got it: Blondies shine when they highlight ingredients that get muted by chocolate. I love chocolate, but let's be honest—it likes to steal the show. For my version of blondies, I decided to completely nix chocolate and focus on a few of my other favorite ingredients: brown butter, brown sugar, and espresso. Toasted hazelnuts add extra texture to these chewy, rich bars.

Preheat the oven to 350°F (175°C) with a rack in the middle.

Spread the hazelnuts on a baking sheet and bake for about 10 minutes, or until fragrant and blistered. Shake the pan a few times for even toasting. Leave the oven on. Wrap the nuts in a clean, lint-free kitchen towel and let steam for 1 to 2 minutes. Rub the nuts against themselves to remove the skins (a few little bits are fine, but try to remove as much as possible). Let the nuts cool completely, then finely chop and set aside.

Line an 8 x 8–inch (20 x 20–cm) pan with foil or parchment, leaving about 3 inches (7.5 cm) of overhang, and lightly grease.

In a large bowl, whisk together the sugars and the salt.

Place the butter in a small, light-colored saucepan over medium-low heat. Once the butter has melted, turn the heat up to medium-high. Stir frequently with a heatproof spatula, scraping the sides and bottom of the pan as needed. The butter will crackle, foam, turn clear gold, then finally start browning. It's done when the crackling subsides and you smell toasted nuts. This process takes about 10 minutes total, but the butter can go from browned to burnt in a flash—so keep an eye on it.

Scrape the butter and all the toasty bits over the sugar mixture. Whisk vigorously to combine. It may look a little clumpy and not completely smooth—that's fine. Add the egg and egg yolk, and whisk vigorously for 1 to 2 minutes or until the mixture is slightly thickened and lighter in color. Whisk in the brewed espresso, espresso powder, and vanilla. Gently whisk in the flour just to combine. Fold in the hazelnuts. Use a flexible spatula to fold from the bottom of the bowl to make sure everything is well mixed and there are no pockets of unincorporated flour.

Pour the batter into the prepared pan and garnish with the flaky sea salt, if desired. Bake until the top is cracked and glossy and a toothpick inserted in the middle comes out with a few moist crumbs, about 20 to 25 minutes. It's essential not to overbake blondies or they will be dry and tough. Err on the side of slightly underbaking them to ensure their chewy texture. Cool blondies completely in the pan on a wire rack before slicing. In an airtight container, the blondies will keep at room temperature for up to 5 days or in the freezer for up to 3 months.

VARIATIONS

Bourbon, Chocolate, and Pecan: Omit the espresso powder and replace the brewed coffee or espresso with 30 grams (2 tbsp) of bourbon. Fold in 85 grams (½ cup) of semi- or bittersweet chopped chocolate or chocolate chips and 70 grams (⅔ cup) of toasted, chopped pecans at the end.

Malted White Chocolate: Add 22 grams (2½ tbsp) of malted milk powder with the sugar and fold in 85 grams (½ cup) of chopped white chocolate at the end.

Butterscotch: Fold in 130 grams (¾ cup) of butterscotch chips at the end. Sprinkle the top with flaky salt before baking.

NO-BAKE NANAIMO BARS

MAKES ONE
9 X 9-INCH
(23 X 23-CM) PAN

BISCUIT BASE
200 g (2 cups) graham cracker crumbs

60 g (⅔ cup) unsweetened dried coconut, shredded or desiccated

50 g (½ cup) toasted pecans or walnuts, finely chopped

113 g (½ cup) unsalted butter

50 g (¼ cup) granulated sugar

½ tsp kosher salt

36 g (5 tbsp) Dutch-processed cocoa powder, sifted

1 large egg, lightly beaten

1 tsp pure vanilla extract

CUSTARD FILLING
113 g (½ cup) unsalted butter, at room temperature

20 g (2 tbsp) custard powder, sifted

Pinch of kosher salt

240 g (2 cups) icing sugar, sifted

½ tsp pure vanilla extract

45 g (3 tbsp) heavy cream, plus more if needed

CHOCOLATE TOPPING
170 g (6 oz) good-quality dark chocolate (60–70% cacao), finely chopped

45 g (3 tbsp) heavy cream

28 g (2 tbsp) unsalted butter

I first encountered Nanaimo bars through a Canadian piano teacher, who served them after one of our holiday recitals. It wasn't until years later that I realized that those no-bake, triple layer bars are one of Canada's best kept secrets, ubiquitous at family gatherings and coffee shops across the Great White North but relatively unknown elsewhere. Nanaimo bars are delightful but rich, so I suggest cutting them into small squares and serving alongside a good cup of coffee.

Line a 9 x 9-inch (23 x 23-cm) pan with foil, dull side up, leaving about 3 inches (7.5 cm) of overhang on two sides. Lightly grease the foil and set aside.

Make the Biscuit Base: In a large bowl, whisk together the graham cracker crumbs, coconut, and pecans. Set aside.

In a small saucepan, melt the butter over low heat. Whisk in the sugar, salt, and cocoa. Heat over low, whisking constantly, until smooth and well combined. Remove from heat. Add the beaten egg and vanilla, whisking furiously all the while to keep the mixture from curdling.

Mix until the mixture is homogenous, then return to low heat. Cook, still whisking constantly, until the mixture is smooth, shiny, and resembles hot fudge, about 1 to 2 minutes. Remove from the heat and pour over the graham cracker mixture. Stir until well combined.

Scrape the mixture into the prepared pan and press firmly to create an even layer. (I like to use the bottom of a small glass or measuring cup to do this.) Refrigerate until firm, about 45 to 60 minutes.

Make the Custard Filling: In the bowl of a stand mixer fitted with the paddle attachment, combine the butter, custard powder, and salt. Beat on medium until smooth and creamy, about 3 minutes. Add the icing sugar in two batches, beating well after each addition. Add the vanilla and cream and beat until smooth and well combined. The mixture should be thick but spreadable—add more cream to adjust the consistency, if needed. Scrape over the chilled biscuit base, using an offset spatula to create a smooth and even layer. Freeze until firm and well chilled, about 20 minutes.

Make the Chocolate Topping: In a heat-safe bowl set over 1 inch (2.5 cm) of gently simmering water, combine the chocolate, cream, and butter. Heat until melted and smooth, stirring frequently. Remove from the heat. Pour over the chilled custard layer, tilting the pan and/or using an offset spatula to create a smooth, even top. Chill until set, about 30 minutes.

To Serve: Lift the excess foil to remove the bars from the pan. Use a sharp chef's knife to cut the bars into squares, cleaning the knife after each cut to ensure clean slices. Serve at room temperature or slightly chilled. Refrigerate leftovers in an airtight container for up to 2 weeks or freeze for up to 3 months.

VARIATIONS

Coffee: In the middle layer, add 4 grams (2 tsp) of espresso powder to the butter, custard powder, and salt. In the top layer, add 1 teaspoon of espresso powder to the rest of the ingredients.

Peppermint: In the middle layer, replace the vanilla with ½ teaspoon of pure peppermint extract. Garnish the bars with crushed peppermint candies.

Triple Chocolate: Substitute chocolate wafer crumbs (such as chocolate graham crackers or OREO® cookies, minus the filling) for the graham cracker crumbs in the bottom layer. In the middle layer, add 12 grams (1½ tbsp) of Dutch-processed cocoa powder to the butter, custard powder, and salt.

Peanut Butter: In the bottom layer, replace the walnuts or pecans with roasted, finely chopped peanuts. In the middle layer, reduce the butter to 28 grams (2 tbsp). Add 120 grams (½ cup) of smooth peanut butter with the butter, custard powder, and salt. Garnish the bars with chopped roasted peanuts.

BAKER'S NOTES

The middle layer of Nanaimo bars gets its signature yellow hue from custard powder. Bird's Custard is a popular brand and easy to find these days, but if your supermarket doesn't carry it, try a British store or online supplier. In a pinch, you can substitute an equal amount of vanilla pudding mix.

MATCHA SHORTBREAD,
ANY WAY YOU SLICE IT

**MAKES ABOUT
24–36 COOKIES,
DEPENDING ON
HOW YOU SLICE IT**

227 g (1 cup) unsalted butter, at
room temperature

80 g (⅔ cup) icing sugar

8 g (1½ tbsp) culinary-grade matcha
powder

1 tsp kosher salt

10 g (2 tsp) pure vanilla extract

250 g (2 cups) all-purpose flour

With its long shelf life and minimal ingredient list—just butter, flour, sugar, and salt for the classic version—shortbread deserves a place in every baker's repertoire. While delightful in its pure and basic form, shortbread is also the perfect blank canvas to experiment with flavors. I'm especially fond of making matcha shortbread as the earthy, herbaceous flavor of the tea really shines through.

In the bowl of a stand mixer fitted with the paddle attachment, combine the butter, sugar, matcha powder, and salt. Mix on low to combine, then increase the speed to medium and beat until smooth and well combined, about 2 to 3 minutes. Scrape down the paddle and sides of the bowl. Add the vanilla and beat well to combine. Turn the mixer down to low and add the flour, mixing just to combine. Use a flexible spatula to fold from the bottom of the bowl to make sure there are no pockets of unincorporated flour. If the dough is very soft and sticky, cover and chill for about 10 minutes before proceeding.

For Slice-and-Bake Shortbread: Divide the dough in half, about 280 grams of dough per half. Place each piece on a piece of plastic wrap and roll into logs about 6 inches (15 cm) long. Wrap tightly in plastic and chill until firm, at least 4 hours. To shape, use a sharp knife to slice each log into 12 to 15 equal rounds, rotating the log a quarter turn after each slice to maintain a round shape. Place the cookies on the prepared baking sheets about 1 inch (2.5 cm) apart. Chill while the oven is preheating.

For Shortbread Fingers: Divide the dough in half, about 280 grams of dough per half. Transfer one half to a piece of parchment paper and roll into a 6-inch (15-cm) square about ½ inch (1.3 cm) thick, using a bench scraper to keep the edges of the dough sharp and straight. Repeat with the other half of the dough. Slide one sheet of the dough onto a baking sheet (still sandwiched between pieces of parchment) and slide the second sheet of dough on top. Refrigerate until firm, at least 30 minutes. To shape, slice each square into twelve 3 x 1-inch (7.5 x 2.5-cm) fingers and prick the tops with a fork, if desired. Chill while the oven is preheating.

For Cutout Cookies: Divide the dough in half, about 280 grams of dough per half. Transfer one half to a piece of parchment paper and pat into a square about 1 inch (2.5 cm) thick. Place another piece of parchment on top and roll dough to about ¼ inch (6 mm) thick, lifting the top piece of parchment occasionally to avoid creases in the dough. Repeat with the other half of the dough. Slide one sheet of the dough onto a baking sheet (still sandwiched between pieces of parchment) and slide the second sheet of dough on top. Refrigerate until firm, at least 30 minutes. Use a cookie cutter to cut shapes as desired, gathering and rerolling the scraps until the dough is used up. Chill while the oven is preheating.

To Bake: Preheat the oven to 325°F (160°C) and line one or two baking sheets with parchment paper. Place the cookies on the prepared baking sheets about 1½ inches (4 cm) apart. Bake until the tops of the cookies are dry and the edges are set, about 15 to 18 minutes for cutout cookies and 23 to 28 for fingers or slice-and-bake.

VARIATIONS

Chocolate Drizzle: For extra flair, melt 170 grams (1 cup) of chocolate (whatever kind you prefer) and drizzle over the baked and cooled cookies. Sprinkle on sesame seeds before the chocolate sets, if desired.

Vanilla: Omit the matcha. Increase the vanilla extract to 15 grams (1 tbsp). For an even fuller vanilla flavor, add the seeds of 1 vanilla bean in with the butter.

Citrus-Poppyseed: Omit the matcha. Add 1½ teaspoons of citrus zest in with the butter and 27 grams (3 tbsp) of poppyseeds with the flour.

Nut: Omit the matcha. Add up to 60 grams (½ cup) of toasted and finely chopped nuts with the flour.

Buckwheat and Cacao Nib: Omit the matcha. Replace 42 grams (⅓ cup) of all-purpose flour with buckwheat flour and mix in 40 grams (⅓ cup) of cacao nibs at the end.

BAKER'S NOTES

Shortbread cookies will keep in an airtight container at room temperature for up to a month, though their color will fade with time.

Using good quality matcha powder will make all the difference in this recipe. Look for 100 percent pure matcha with a vibrant green color, preferably culinary grade, at your local Asian supermarket or online supplier.

RHUBARB *and* WALNUT LINZER COOKIES

MAKES ABOUT
30 SANDWICH COOKIES

WALNUT LINZER COOKIES
105 g (scant 1 cup) chopped walnuts, toasted and cooled
75 g (⅓ cup plus 2 tsp) granulated sugar
75 g (⅓ cup plus 2 tsp) light brown sugar
1 tsp kosher salt
281 g (2¼ cups) all-purpose flour
227 g (1 cup) unsalted butter, cold and cubed
1 large egg, cold
1 large egg yolk, cold
10 g (2 tsp) pure vanilla extract

RHUBARB JAM
250 g (2 cups) rhubarb, chopped
100 g (½ cup) granulated sugar
Generous pinch of kosher salt
½ tsp pure vanilla extract
Juice of ½ a lemon

Linzer cookies make a stunning addition to holiday cookie spreads, but these delightful sandwich cookies deserve to be enjoyed year-round. Raspberry preserves and almond-enriched dough are traditional Linzer fare, but here I've switched things up with a tart rhubarb jam and toasty walnuts.

Make the Walnut Linzer Cookie Dough: In the bowl of a food processor, combine the walnuts, sugars, and salt. Pulse together until the nuts are finely ground and the mixture is the texture of damp sand. Add the flour and pulse to combine. Scatter the butter cubes over the top and pulse until the butter is well incorporated, with no large pieces remaining. Scrape down the sides of the food processor a couple times during this process.

In a separate bowl, whisk together the egg, egg yolk, and vanilla. Drizzle over the flour mixture and process in 10-second pulses just until a dough starts to form. Transfer about half of the dough to a piece of plastic wrap. Pat into a square about 1 inch (2.5 cm) thick. Place another piece of plastic wrap on top and roll the dough to about ³⁄₁₆ inch (5 mm). Lift and replace the top piece of plastic occasionally to avoid creases in the dough. Repeat with the other half of the dough. Slide one sheet of the dough onto a baking sheet (still sandwiched between pieces of plastic) and slide the second sheet of dough on top. Refrigerate until cold, about 3 hours or up to 24 hours.

Make the Rhubarb Jam: Combine the rhubarb, sugar, salt, vanilla, and lemon juice in a medium saucepan. Cook, stirring frequently, over medium-high heat until boiling. Reduce the heat to medium and continue cooking, stirring frequently, until the mixture is thick and sticky, about 20 to 30 minutes. Transfer to a clean jar and cool to room temperature. Refrigerate until ready to use.

Bake and Assemble the Cookies: Preheat the oven to 350°F (175°C) with a rack in the middle and line two baking sheets with parchment paper. Remove one sheet of the dough from the fridge. Peel off the top piece of plastic, invert the dough onto one of the parchment-lined baking sheets, and peel off the other piece of plastic. Use a 2½-inch (6-cm) round cookie cutter to punch out as many rounds as possible. Remove the excess dough and set aside. Repeat with the second sheet of dough. Use a small round cutter to punch out the centers of half of the circles. Chill the cut cookies until firm, about 15 minutes. Reroll and repeat the cutting process with the dough scraps, chilling as necessary.

Bake the sheets one at a time for about 15 minutes, or until the cookies are just barely golden on the edges. Cool the cookies on the sheet for 5 minutes before transferring to a wire rack to cool completely.

Sift the icing sugar over the cookies with the center cut-outs. Using a small spoon or offset spatula, spread about 1 teaspoon of the Rhubarb Jam on the flat sides of the bottom cookies. Top each with a sugared cookie. Serve immediately, or store in an airtight container between layers of parchment or wax paper until serving.

VARIATIONS

Nut Swap: Replace the walnuts with an equal weight of toasted almonds, pistachios, or pecans.

Alternate Fillings: Replace the Rhubarb Jam with another thick jam, fruit curd, salted caramel, chocolate ganache, or Nutella.

Thumbprint Cookies: Instead of rolling out the dough, portion it into roughly 1-tablespoon balls. Place the balls on the prepared baking sheets 2 inches (5 cm) apart. Make an indent in each one using the handle of a wooden spoon or your thumb and chill until firm. Bake at 350°F (175°C) until lightly golden, about 15 minutes, reinforcing the indent halfway through baking if needed. After the cookies have cooled, fill the indent with filling of choice.

BAKER'S NOTES

You can bake these cookies several days in advance (store them at room temperature in an airtight container), but I recommend filling them on the day you plan to serve them as the cookies will gradually soften once they're filled.

CRANBERRY & PISTACHIO CRISPS

MAKES ABOUT
6 DOZEN CRISPS

250 g (2 cups) white whole-wheat flour
9 g (2 tsp) baking soda
6 g (1½ tsp) kosher salt
480 g (2 cups) buttermilk, at room temperature
50 g (¼ cup) brown sugar (light or dark)
80 g (¼ cup) honey
50 g (½ cup) chopped pistachios
30 g (¼ cup) pepitas
120 g (1 cup) dried cranberries
50 g (¼ cup) millet
35 g (¼ cup) sesame seeds
28 g (3 tbsp) ground flax seed
2 g (1 tbsp) fresh thyme, chopped

Nutty, fruity, savory, and sweet, these addictive crisps are an excellent addition to a nosh plate or cheeseboard. Every time I've brought them to share, people are shocked that they aren't store-bought. The truth is, these crackers are so easy to make that once you try, you'll likely swear off buying them. I especially like making and freezing a few batches around the holidays, baking them off as needed for parties or gifting.

Preheat the oven to 350°F (175°C) with a rack in the middle. Lightly grease four mini (5¾ x 3¼ x 2¼-inch [15 x 8 x 6-cm]) loaf pans.

In a large bowl, whisk together the flour, baking soda, and salt. Whisk in the buttermilk, brown sugar, and honey. Add in the pistachios, pepitas, cranberries, millet, sesame seeds, flax seed, and thyme, mixing just until evenly combined.

Divide the batter evenly between the prepared pans, about 290 grams (2⅓ cups) per pan. Place the mini loaf pans on a baking sheet and bake until the loaves are golden and springy to the touch, about 30 minutes. Immediately turn the loaves out of their pans and cool completely on a wire rack. For easiest slicing, chill the loaves completely (about 2 hours in the fridge does the trick).

Using a sharp serrated knife, slice the loaves crosswise as thinly as you can and place the slices in a single layer on ungreased baking sheets. Meanwhile, preheat the oven to 300°F (150°C) with racks in the upper and lower thirds.

Bake the slices for about 15 minutes, then flip them over and bake for another 10 to 15 minutes, until crisp and deeply golden. If the slices are not quite crisp at this point (but are already deeply colored), turn off the heat and leave in the oven with the door cracked open for an extra 10 to 15 minutes to dry, checking every 5 minutes or so. Cool the crisps completely on a wire rack, then store in an airtight container for up to 2 months.

VARIATIONS

Holiday Spice Blend: Add ½ teaspoon of ground cinnamon, ½ teaspoon of ground ginger, and ¼ teaspoon each of ground nutmeg, cloves, and allspice in with the flour mixture. Replace the honey with 80 grams (¼ cup) of mild (fancy) molasses.

Chocolate-Orange: Reduce the flour to 219 grams (1¾ cups) and add 20 grams (¼ cup) of unsweetened cocoa powder. Replace the pepitas with 30 grams (¼ cup) of cacao nibs. Add the zest of an orange and ½ teaspoon each of ground cinnamon and ground cardamom in with the flour mixture.

Sourdough Discard: Reduce the flour to 188 grams (1½ cups) and the buttermilk to 360 grams (1½ cups). Whisk 227 grams (1 cup) of sourdough starter (100 percent hydration, fed or unfed) with the buttermilk and add to the dry ingredients along with the sugar and honey.

Fruit and Nut Swaps: Replace the dried cranberries and pistachios with your favorite dried fruit and nuts. Some favorite combinations include fig and hazelnut, raisin and almond, or cherry and pecan. Chop both if large and lightly toast the nuts if desired.

BAKER'S NOTES

If you don't have mini loaf pans (or want longer crisps), you can bake the batter in two 8½ x 4½-inch (22 x 11–cm) loaf pans for about 45 minutes.

If you don't want to bake off all the crackers at once, wrap the cooled loaves in plastic and freeze for up to 3 months. Slice and bake straight from the freezer.

CHOCOLATE–ALMOND BISCOTTI

MAKES 3–4 DOZEN
BISCOTTI

110 g (½ cup) neutral vegetable oil, such as grapeseed or canola

3 large eggs, cold

200 g (1 cup) granulated sugar

8 g (1½ tsp) pure almond extract

8 g (1½ tsp) pure vanilla extract

400 g (3¼ cups) all-purpose flour

12 g (1 tbsp) baking powder

¾ tsp kosher salt

170 g (1 cup) semi-sweet chocolate chips

140 g (1 cup) toasted almonds, roughly chopped

When I became serious about learning to bake, one of the first recipes I tackled was biscotti. I liked that they didn't require a ton of ingredients, had an incredible shelf life, and looked a little fancy without too much effort. My husband would take batches to work to enjoy during coffee breaks, and I knew I was on to something when he mentioned that an Italian colleague frequently dropped by his desk to raid the biscotti stash, claiming, with a knowing smile, that they were nearly as good as her own. I like chocolate and almonds in my biscotti, but these versatile twice-baked cookies are easily adapted to showcase different flavor profiles or your favorite mix-ins.

Preheat the oven to 375°F (190°C) with a rack in the middle. Line a large baking sheet with parchment paper.

In a large bowl, whisk together the oil, eggs, sugar, and extracts until smooth. In a separate bowl, whisk together the flour, baking powder, and salt.

Pour the dry ingredients into the wet and use a flexible spatula or wooden spoon to gently combine.

When the dry ingredients are almost fully incorporated, mix in the chocolate chips and almonds. Stir just until everything is evenly combined and there are no streaks of flour remaining. Cover the bowl and chill the dough for about 15 minutes for easier handling.

Divide the dough into halves, about 618 grams each. Transfer the halves to the prepared baking sheet and, using damp hands, pat into logs about 12 x 4 inches (30 x 10 cm) and about ¾ inch (2 cm) thick. Use a damp bench scraper to smooth the tops. Place the logs on the prepared baking sheet at least 3 inches (7.5 cm) apart, as they will spread a little during baking.

Bake until the edges are lightly golden and the top is firm and beginning to crack, about 25 to 30 minutes. Transfer the sheet to a wire rack and cool for about 20 to 30 minutes, or until the logs are cool enough to handle but still slightly warm. Don't cool too long, or the biscotti will be more prone to crumble when slicing. Meanwhile, reduce the oven temperature to 350°F (175°C).

Carefully transfer one log at a time to a cutting board. Use a sharp serrated knife to slice each log crosswise into ½- to ¾-inch (1.3- to 2-cm) pieces. Place the cookies back on the baking sheet, cut side up, and bake for about 10 to 12 minutes, until lightly browned and dry to the touch. Flip the cookies over and bake for another 10 to 12 minutes.

Cool completely on a wire rack before serving (biscotti will crisp up as they cool). Store leftover biscotti at room temperature in an airtight container for up to 3 months.

VARIATIONS

Almond-Anise: For a traditional almond-anise biscotti, add 7 grams (1 tbsp) of crushed anise seed to the dry ingredients. Omit the chocolate chips and increase the toasted, chopped almonds to 210 grams (1½ cups). Replace the vanilla with 1 teaspoon of anise extract.

Chocolate Drizzle: For extra flair, drizzle the twice-baked, completely cooled biscotti with 227 grams (1½ cups) of melted chocolate.

Whole-Wheat: Replace up to half of the flour with white whole-wheat or sifted whole-wheat flour.

Butter Pecan: Omit the almond extract and increase the vanilla to 15 grams (1 tbsp). Replace the almonds with toasted, chopped pecans and the chocolate chips with butterscotch chips.

Choose-Your-Own Mix-Ins: This recipe can accommodate up to 450 grams (3 cups) of mix-ins such as dried fruit, chopped nuts, and chocolate chips. Swap in your favorite combinations and adjust the extracts and spices to complement, if desired.

BAKER'S NOTES

Depending on the size of your baking sheets and how thick you cut your biscotti, you may need to use more than one baking sheet for the second round of baking. You can either bake the sheets one at a time or place racks in the upper and lower thirds of your oven and bake both at once, swapping the positions of the sheets when you flip the biscotti over.

BERRY SWIRL MERINGUE CLOUDS

MAKES 12 MERINGUES

QUICK BERRY JAM
113 g (4 oz) fresh or frozen berries
28 g (2 tbsp) granulated sugar
Pinch of salt
Squeeze of lemon or lime juice

MERINGUES
120 g (½ cup) egg whites (from about 4 large eggs), at room temperature
¼ tsp cream of tartar
¼ tsp kosher salt
200 g (1 cup) granulated sugar, preferably caster or superfine (see Baker's Notes)
5 g (2 tsp) cornstarch, sifted
1 tsp pure vanilla extract
1 tsp lemon juice or vinegar

There's something magical about making meringue. I love watching the simple combination of egg whites and sugar transform from a puddle of liquid into beautiful billows. You can pipe meringue into any number of shapes and sizes, but I think it's most charming to simply dollop it into rustic cloud-like shapes. In this recipe, a ribbon of berry jam adds a little tang to temper the sweetness, not to mention a beautiful splash of color.

Make the Quick Berry Jam: Combine the berries, sugar, salt, and lemon juice in a medium saucepan and bring to a boil over medium heat, stirring and smashing the berries occasionally with a heatproof spatula. Once the mixture reaches a boil, continue cooking for about 5 to 10 minutes, stirring frequently, until thickened. Strain the jam into a heatproof container to remove any seeds and cool to room temperature. Refrigerate the jam until ready to use.

Make the Meringues: Preheat the oven to 200°F (95°C) and line one large or two medium baking sheets with parchment paper. Trace twelve 3-inch (7.5-cm) circles about 2 inches (5 cm) apart on the parchment paper. Turn the parchment paper over so you don't get pen marks on the meringues.

Combine the egg whites, cream of tartar, and salt in the bowl of a stand mixer fitted with the whisk attachment. Whisk on low to combine, then turn the speed up to medium and whip until frothy. With the mixer is still running, slowly add the sugar 1 teaspoon at a time, waiting about 10 seconds between each addition. Once all the sugar has been added, turn the speed up to high and whip until the meringue is glossy, thick, and holds stiff peaks, about 3 minutes. Rub a little of the meringue between your fingers. It should feel smooth with no grittiness from the sugar. If not, continue whisking until the sugar is completely dissolved.

Sprinkle the cornstarch, vanilla, and lemon juice on top and use a flexible spatula to fold gently to combine.

Divide the meringue into 12 equal rounds, using a cookie or ice cream scoop or two spoons, using the pre-drawn circles as a guide.

Dollop a scant teaspoon of the Quick Berry Jam on top of each meringue and use a skewer or knife to gently swirl it around.

Bake the meringues for 2 hours, then turn the oven off and allow the meringues to cool gradually inside the oven for at least an hour (or up to overnight). When baking meringues, think "low and slow"—you're not so much baking them as drying them out. The low temperature also helps preserve the snowy white color. If your meringues start to take on color, try lowering the temperature by 15 to 20°F (10 to 15°C) and baking longer. Store leftover meringues in an airtight container at room temperature for up to 5 days.

VARIATIONS

Extracts and Oils: Swap out the vanilla for another pure extract or oil such as almond, lemon, peppermint, coconut, rosewater, or orange blossom water. Less is more with these flavors, so start with a small amount and add more to taste.

Extra Fruity: Fold 8 grams (2 tbsp) of finely ground freeze-dried berries—or up to 18 grams (1 cup) of larger bits, if you prefer some texture—before portioning the meringues.

Chocolate Swirl: Omit the berry swirl. Before making the meringue, melt 100 grams (scant ⅔ cup) of chopped dark chocolate. Before scooping the meringues, drizzle in about ¾ of the melted chocolate and fold a few times just to distribute. Portion the meringues as directed, then drizzle the remaining chocolate on top.

BAKER'S NOTES

Make sure your mixer bowl, whisk attachment, and spatula are grease-free before starting, otherwise the egg whites won't whip up properly. I like to use a bit of lemon juice to wipe down all my equipment before starting as a precaution.

Caster or superfine sugar is recommended for meringues, because the small granules dissolve more quickly than regular granulated sugar. If you can't find superfine or caster sugar easily, you can make your own by grinding granulated sugar in a food processor for about 1 minute.

TUCK IT IN A CRUST: PIES, TARTS, & GALETTES

I love making pies, tarts, and galettes throughout the year. Tucking just about anything into a crust instantly makes it feel more special—be it seasonal fruit, veggies and cheese, or chocolate and caramel.

The first step to pie and tart success is having one or two reliable crust recipes. In this chapter, I share my favorites, such as the All-Butter Pie Crust (page 52), along with tips and tricks to make the whole crust-making process enjoyable and stress-free.

Once you have your crust sorted, it's time to choose a delicious filling. For something quick and fuss-free, try the Tomato and Ricotta Galette (page 52) or one of its several variations. Either the Mango and Strawberry Cream Tart (page 66) or the Chocolate Caramel Pretzel Tart (page 72) make an elegant finish to a dinner party. Or break out a classic Pumpkin Pie with Brown Butter Pecan Streusel (page 60) for your next holiday spread.

Whether you're a pie newbie or a seasoned professional, I hope the following recipes and variations will inspire you to dive deep into the world of pies, tarts, and galettes. It's one of the most delicious worlds I know, and the creative possibilities—both sweet and savory—are truly endless!

TOMATO *and* RICOTTA GALETTE

MAKES ONE
9– TO 10–INCH
(23– TO 25–CM)
GALETTE

**ALL–BUTTER PIE CRUST
(MAKES 2 CRUSTS)**
250 g (2 cups) all-purpose flour
125 g (1 cup) whole-grain flour
(such as whole-wheat, spelt,
kamut, or rye)
6 g (1½ tsp) kosher salt
12 g (1 tbsp) granulated sugar
250 g (1 cup plus 2 tbsp) unsalted
butter, cold and cut into ½-inch
(1.25-cm) cubes
120 g (½ cup) ice water, as needed

Galettes are the cool, casual cousin of the pie family. Essentially a single-crust, freeform pie baked on a baking sheet instead of a pie plate, they're easy to make and celebrated for their rustic charm. While galettes can be made and enjoyed year-round, I make them most often during the summer when there's an abundance of fresh produce and I don't have the time to invest in a full-blown pie. This savory galette is especially delicious in late summer during peak tomato season, but you can easily adapt this recipe to use whatever vegetables you have on hand. The pie crust recipe makes enough for two galettes (or two single-crust pies or one double-crust pie); extra dough can be frozen, well wrapped in plastic, for up to 3 months. Thaw overnight in the fridge before using.

Make the All-Butter Pie Crust: In a large bowl, whisk together the flours, salt, and sugar. Scatter the butter over the top. Use the pads of your fingers to flatten the butter pieces, tossing them with the flour mixture so each piece is coated on all sides. The butter pieces should remain fairly large, about the size of walnut halves. Work quickly so the butter remains cold.

Drizzle about 75 grams (5 tbsp) of the ice water over the flour-butter mixture and use a fork or your hands to "toss" the two together, similar to the way you would dress salad greens. Add water, 1 or 2 teaspoons at a time, tossing after each addition, until the dough just holds together when you squeeze a bit in your hand. (I usually need 120 to 150 grams [8 to 10 tbsp] total, but the amount can vary depending on the flour you're using and the humidity.)

Fold the dough over itself several times, giving the bowl a quarter turn after each fold, to make a cohesive but ragged mass. You should still see visible pieces of butter—this is a good thing! Transfer the dough to a piece of plastic wrap and pat into a rectangle. Wrap to seal, then use your hands or a rolling pin to flatten the dough to about ¾ inch (2 cm) thick. Refrigerate for 30 minutes.

Transfer the chilled dough to a lightly floured surface. Using a floured rolling pin, roll the dough into a roughly 13-inch (33-cm) square. Brush off any extra flour and fold the dough into thirds like a letter. Fold into thirds again so you end up with a roughly 4½-inch (11-cm) square. Roll into a ¾-inch (2-cm)-thick rectangle twice as long as it is wide and cut in half. Use your hands to round the edges of each half into a disc. Wrap each half and refrigerate for at least 2 hours, or up to 2 days. (The dough can also be frozen at this point and defrosted in the fridge overnight before using.)

(Continued)

VARIATIONS

Veggie and Cheese Swaps: Substitute the tomato slices with an equal amount of sliced zucchini or eggplant (following the same steps for salting and draining any extra liquid), asparagus spears, or about 1½ cups of sautéed mushrooms, leeks, or leafy greens (drain any excess liquid before assembly). Substitute the ricotta with an equal amount of cottage cheese, fresh goat cheese, or mascarpone.

Fig, Onion, and Labneh: Replace the ricotta filling with 120 grams (½ cup) of labneh mixed with the finely chopped shallot and salt and pepper to taste. Top with 1 large onion, thinly sliced, sautéed until soft and golden, and seasoned with salt and pepper. Replace the tomato slices with about 12 medium-sized fresh figs, halved or quartered, and arranged cut side up. Bake as directed. Garnish with flaky salt, fresh thyme leaves, and a drizzle of balsamic vinegar, if desired.

Plum and Honey Frangipane: Replace the ricotta filling with honey frangipane. To make the frangipane, cream together 42 grams (3 tbsp) of softened unsalted butter, 70 grams (3½ tbsp) of honey, a dash of pure vanilla extract, a pinch of salt, and 1 large egg. Fold in 75 grams (¾ cup) of almond flour and 12 grams (2 tbsp) of all-purpose flour. Replace the tomato slices with plum slices. Sprinkle the galette with coarse sugar before baking. Bake as directed. Serve with an extra drizzle of honey.

BAKER'S NOTES

I always use a portion of whole-grain flour in my pie crusts, because I love the added depth of flavor. I use whatever whole grains I have on hand, often a mix—though I'm partial to spelt. You can replace the whole-grain flour with more all-purpose flour if you prefer.

RICOTTA FILLING

120 g (½ cup) ricotta cheese

33 g (⅓ cup) Parmesan cheese, freshly grated

I small shallot, finely diced

15 g (1 tbsp) Dijon mustard

Salt and pepper, to taste

TO FINISH

340 g (¾ lb) ripe but firm tomatoes, preferably heirloom (about 2–3 medium)

½ tsp kosher salt

I large egg, whisked with 1 tsp milk or water and a pinch of salt, for egg wash

Flaky salt and pepper, for sprinkling

Olive oil, for drizzling

Fresh basil leaves or finely chopped chives, for garnishing (optional)

Make the Ricotta Filling: Mix the ricotta, Parmesan, shallot, and mustard until smooth. Season with salt and pepper and set aside.

Assemble and Bake the Galette: Preheat the oven to 400°F (200°C) with a rack in the middle.

Cut the tomatoes into ¼-inch (6-mm)-thick slices and spread in an even layer on a cutting board or plate. Sprinkle with the salt. Let sit for 15 minutes to allow the juices to release.

Remove one disc of the chilled pie dough from the fridge and let it stand for about 5 to 10 minutes, just long enough to make it pliable. (You will only need one crust for the galette, so the second disc can be frozen or used for another recipe.) On a floured surface, roll into a 13- to 14-inch (33- to 36-cm) round just under ¼ inch (6 mm) thick. Roll from the center out, giving the dough a quarter turn after every roll to avoid sticking and ensure an even thickness. Use kitchen shears to trim the edges to neaten, if desired. Dust off any excess flour and transfer, still on the parchment, to a baking sheet.

Spread the ricotta filling evenly over the chilled pie dough, leaving a 2-inch (5-cm) border all around. Drain the extra liquid from the tomatoes and blot them dry with a paper towel. Arrange the tomato slices evenly on top of the cheese. Fold the edges of the dough over the filling, overlapping as you go around. Refrigerate the galette until the pastry is firm, about 20 to 30 minutes.

Right before baking, brush the crust with the egg wash. Generously sprinkle the top of the entire galette with flaky salt and pepper, and drizzle the tomatoes with olive oil.

Bake until the crust is deeply golden and the tomatoes are cooked, about 40 to 45 minutes. Transfer to a wire rack and cool for about 10 minutes. Garnish with fresh basil or chives, if desired. Serve warm or at room temperature. The galette is best served the day it is baked. Refrigerate leftovers in an airtight container for up to 3 days.

BLUEBERRY–LEMON SOUR CREAM PIE

MAKES ONE 9-INCH (23-CM) PIE

BLIND-BAKED PIE CRUST
½ batch All-Butter Pie Crust (page 52)

Pie weights, dried beans, rice, or sugar, for blind-baking

LEMON–SOUR CREAM FILLING
57 g (¼ cup) unsalted butter, cold

200 g (1 cup) sugar

Zest of 3 lemons

36 g (¼ cup plus 1 tbsp) cornstarch

¼ tsp kosher salt

240 g (1 cup) whole milk

120 g (½ cup) freshly squeezed lemon juice (from about 2–3 large lemons)

3 large egg yolks

240 g (1 cup) sour cream

BLUEBERRY TOPPING
340 g (2⅓ cups) fresh blueberries

8 g (1 tbsp) arrowroot starch (cornstarch can be substituted, but arrowroot creates a clearer glaze)

50 g (¼ cup) granulated sugar

120 g (½ cup) water

8 g (1½ tsp) freshly squeezed lemon juice

TO FINISH
240 grams (1 cup) heavy whipping cream, whipped into stiff peaks

As a kid, one of my favorite desserts was a blueberry sour cream pie from a local restaurant. A tart and luscious lemon custard topped with a pile of fresh blueberries, all tucked into a buttery crust and finished with whipped cream—what's not to love? This creamy crowd-pleaser is a fresh alternative to lemon meringue pie, and the no-bake, make-ahead stovetop filling makes this pie perfect for entertaining.

Prepare the Blind-Baked Pie Crust: Remove the chilled pie dough from the fridge and let it stand for about 5 to 10 minutes, just long enough to make it pliable. On a floured surface, roll the dough into a 13-inch (33-cm) round just under ¼ inch (6 mm) thick. Roll from the center out, giving the dough a quarter turn after every roll to avoid sticking and ensure an even thickness. Dust off any excess flour.

Carefully roll the dough onto the rolling pin and unfurl into a standard 9-inch (23-cm) pie plate. Gently lift the edges and press the dough into the bottom and sides of the plate, being careful not to stretch the dough to fit. Trim the overhang to 1 inch (2.5 cm) all around, then fold the excess dough under itself to form a border. The edge should be flush with the pie plate. Prick the bottom of the dough several times with a fork. Crimp the edges as desired. Cover and chill until the pastry is firm, at least 30 minutes or up to 24 hours.

Preheat the oven to 375°F (190°C) with a rack in the lower third. To blind-bake the crust, place the chilled pie crust on a foil-lined baking sheet. Take a piece of foil that is slightly larger than the pie plate and carefully press it into the chilled pie crust, dull side down. Fill the crust with pie weights of your choice, all the way up to the crimp. Bake the crust for about 30 minutes, or until the crimps are set.

Remove the pie plate from the oven and carefully lift out the foil and pie weights. Return the crust to the oven and bake for another 10 to 20 minutes, or until the crust is evenly browned. Remove and cool on a wire rack until ready to fill (no need to cool it completely).

(Continued)

Make the Lemon–Sour Cream Filling: Cube the butter and place it in a large heat-safe bowl. Set a sieve over the bowl.

Combine the sugar, lemon zest, cornstarch, and salt in a medium saucepan and whisk until combined. Whisk in the milk, lemon juice, and egg yolks.

Set the saucepan over medium-low heat and cook, whisking constantly, until steaming. Raise the heat to medium and continue to cook and whisk until the mixture thickens and large bubbles begin appearing on the surface. Once the large bubbles appear, continue whisking on the heat for 2 minutes longer.

Remove from the heat and strain into the bowl with the butter. Whisk to combine. Allow the mixture to cool, whisking occasionally, for about 30 minutes. Whisk in the sour cream, then scrape the filling into the pre-baked crust. Refrigerate at least 4 hours to set the filling.

Make the Blueberry Topping: Rinse and dry the blueberries and place in a large bowl and set aside.

In a medium saucepan, whisk together the arrowroot starch and sugar. Whisk in the water and lemon juice. Place the saucepan over medium heat, whisking constantly, until the glaze is clear and thickened. Remove from the heat and add the blueberries, tossing to coat.

Drain the berry mixture in a colander or sieve to remove any excess glaze. Cool to room temperature before topping the pie.

Assemble the Pie: Just before serving, pipe or spread the whipped cream on top of the chilled lemon filling and spoon on the blueberry topping. The pie is best served the day it is made. Refrigerate leftovers in an airtight container for up to 3 days.

VARIATIONS

Crust Variations: Replace the All-Butter Pie Crust with a Graham Cracker Crust (page 90). You can also make this recipe as a tart, using the Pâte Sucrée Crust (page 66).

Lime-Blackberry: Use lime zest and juice in place of the lemon and substitute blackberries for blueberries.

Creamy Lemon Meringue: Omit the blueberries and whipped cream. Follow the instructions for making a Vanilla Swiss Meringue Buttercream (page 79), omitting the butter. Spread or pipe on top of the pie. Just before serving, toast with a kitchen torch or place under a preheated medium-high broiler for 1 to 2 minutes, checking often, as the meringue burns easily.

BAKER'S NOTES

Whipped cream is the perfect topping for this pie, but it may begin deflating or weeping after 2 or 3 hours. If you need to make the whipped cream ahead of time, dissolve ½ teaspoon of powdered gelatin in 20 grams (4 tsp) of cold water. Let sit for 5 minutes, then heat for 5 to 10 seconds in the microwave until just melted. Whisk the whipped cream on medium speed until soft peaks begin to form. Turn the mixer down to low and slowly pour in the melted gelatin while continuing to whip. Once the gelatin has been added, turn up the mixer to medium-high and whip until the cream reaches stiff peaks. Stabilized whipped cream will keep in the fridge for 24 hours.

CLASSIC APPLE PIE

MAKES ONE 9–INCH (23–CM)
PIE

**1 batch All-Butter Pie Crust
(page 52)**

APPLE PIE FILLING
2 kg (4½ lbs) apples, peeled, cored,
and sliced ¼ to ⅛ inch
(3 to 6 mm) thick (see Baker's
Notes)
65 g (⅓ cup) brown sugar
50 g (¼ cup) granulated sugar
½ tsp kosher salt
30 g (2 tbsp) freshly squeezed
lemon juice
42 g (⅓ cup) all-purpose flour
5 g (2 tsp) ground cinnamon
1 tsp ground ginger
¼ tsp freshly ground nutmeg

TO FINISH
1 large egg, whisked with 1 tsp milk
or water and a pinch of salt, for egg
wash
Coarse sugar, for garnishing

One of the most memorable early dates with my now-husband was apple picking at a nearby orchard, followed by an evening attempting to bake our first from-scratch apple pie. I don't remember how that pie turned out, but ever since then we've made it a fall tradition to go to the orchard to pick apples and make this pie.

Roll Out the Pie Dough: Remove one disc of the chilled pie dough from the fridge and let it stand until pliable, about 5 to 10 minutes. On a floured surface, roll into a 13-inch (33-cm) round just under ¼ inch (6 mm) thick. Roll from the center out, giving the dough a quarter turn after every roll to avoid sticking and ensure an even thickness. Dust off any excess flour. Carefully roll it onto the rolling pin and unfurl into a standard 9-inch (23-cm) pie plate. Gently lift the edges and press the dough into the bottom and sides of the plate, being careful not to stretch the dough to fit. Trim the overhang to 1 inch (2.5 cm) all around. Remove the other disc of dough from the fridge and roll into a 13-inch (33-cm) round on a lightly floured piece of parchment. Transfer, still on the parchment, to a cutting board or baking sheet. Cover and refrigerate both while you prepare the filling.

Make the Apple Pie Filling: Transfer the apple slices to a large, wide bowl. Sprinkle the sugars and salt over the apple slices and use your hands or a flexible spatula to mix well. Sprinkle the lemon juice over the apples and mix well. Cover and let stand at room temperature for at least 30 minutes, or up to 4 hours, to macerate. When macerated, strain the liquid from the apples into a medium saucepan and return the apples to the large bowl. Simmer the liquid over medium heat until reduced to a syrupy consistency, 6 to 8 minutes, then remove from heat and set aside to cool slightly.

Whisk together the flour, cinnamon, ginger, and nutmeg in a small bowl. Sprinkle over the apples and toss to coat. Pour the cooled, thickened fruit liquid over the apples and gently stir to combine.

Assemble and Bake the Pie: Fill the prepared pie crust with the apple slices by layering and stacking the slices in concentric circles and mounding the apples up more in the center. Once filled, brush the exposed rim of pie dough with water. Remove the second pie crust from the fridge and center it over the filling. Press the edges of the two crusts together, then trim the dough to a 1-inch (2.5-cm) overhang all around. Tuck the overhang under itself and press onto the edges of the pie plate to seal. Crimp the border as desired. Chill the pie until the pastry is firm, about 30 minutes, while the oven preheats. Preheat the oven to 400°F (200°C) with a rack in the lower third. If you have a baking steel or stone, preheat that as well. If not, preheat a large foil-lined baking sheet.

Right before baking, brush the crust with the egg wash and sprinkle generously with coarse sugar. Cut at least four 2-inch (5-cm) vent holes in the top crust. Bake for about 70 to 90 minutes, or until the crust is deeply golden and the juices are bubbling in the center. (Tent the pie with foil partway through baking if the crust is browning too quickly.) A paring knife inserted into one of the vent holes should pierce through the filling without resistance. Remove from the oven and cool to room temperature on a wire rack before slicing, at least 4 hours.

VARIATIONS

Apple-Pear: Replace half of the apple slices with an equal amount of peeled, sliced ripe-but-firm pears (I prefer Bosc or Seckel varieties for baking).

Apple-Cranberry: Reduce the apples to 1.6 kg (3½ lbs) and add 120 grams (1 cup) of fresh cranberries to the filling, adding the cranberries with the flour and spices. Replace the lemon juice with freshly squeezed orange juice. Add the zest of an orange to the spices, if desired.

Caramel Apple: Omit the granulated sugar in the filling. After you've arranged about half of the apple slices into the bottom crust, drizzle the apples with 110 grams (⅓ cup) of cooled Salted Caramel Sauce (page 164). Top with the remaining apple slices, followed by another 110 grams (⅓ cup) of caramel sauce.

Spiced Crust: When making the pie crust, whisk in ½ teaspoon each of ground cinnamon and ground ginger and ¼ teaspoon each of ground nutmeg, ground allspice, and ground cardamom into the flour mixture before adding the butter.

BAKER'S NOTES

I like to use a variety of firm baking apples with differing levels of tartness, such as Mutsu, Northern Spy, Granny Smith, Fuji, and Ambrosia.

Apple pie is best served the day it's baked. Store leftovers in an airtight container at room temperature for up to 2 days.

PUMPKIN PIE *with* BROWN BUTTER PECAN STREUSEL

MAKES ONE 9–INCH (23–CM) PIE

BLIND–BAKED PIE CRUST
½ batch All-Butter Pie Crust (page 52)
Pie weights, dried beans, rice, or sugar, for blind-baking

BROWN BUTTER PECAN STREUSEL
70 g (5 tbsp) unsalted butter
94 g (¾ cup) all-purpose flour
50 g (¼ cup) light brown sugar
50 g (¼ cup) granulated sugar
½ tsp kosher salt
60 g (½ cup) chopped pecans

PUMPKIN PIE FILLING
168 g (¾ cup) heavy cream
125 g (½ cup) whole milk
3 large eggs, at room temperature
1 tsp pure vanilla extract
15 g (1 tbsp) bourbon (optional)
425 g (1¾ cups) pure pumpkin puree
130 g (⅔ cup) light brown sugar
1 tsp ground ginger
1 tsp ground cinnamon
¼ tsp grated nutmeg
¼ tsp ground allspice
¼ tsp ground black pepper
½ tsp kosher salt

I love pumpkin pie. While many people will eat a slice only on Thanksgiving for tradition's sake, I stock up on pumpkin puree when it's on sale to enjoy pumpkin pie year-round. While I'm always up for trying new flavor twists, my favorite is still the classic combination of cinnamon, ginger, nutmeg, and allspice, plus a little black pepper and bourbon for a subtle kick. A brown butter pecan streusel adds an extra layer of flavor and texture, if you can avoid snacking on it straight from the pan.

Prepare the Blind-Baked Crust: Remove one disc of the chilled pie dough from the fridge and let it stand for about 5 to 10 minutes, just long enough to make it pliable. On a floured surface, roll into a 13- to 14-inch (33- to 36-cm) round just under ¼ inch (6 mm) thick. Roll from the center out, giving the dough a quarter turn after every roll to avoid sticking and ensure an even thickness. Dust off any excess flour. Carefully roll the dough onto the rolling pin and unfurl into a standard 9-inch (23-cm) pie plate. Gently lift the edges and press the dough into the bottom and sides of the plate, being careful not to stretch the dough to fit. Trim the overhang to 1 inch (2.5 cm) all around, then fold the excess dough under itself to form a border. The edge should be flush with the pie plate. Prick the bottom of the dough several times with a fork. Crimp the edges as desired. Cover and chill until the pastry is firm, at least 30 minutes or up to 24 hours.

Preheat the oven to 375°F (190°C) with a rack in the lower third. To blind-bake the crust, place the chilled pie crust on a foil-lined baking sheet. Take a piece of foil that is slightly larger than the pie plate and carefully press it into the chilled pie crust, dull side down. Fill the crust with pie weights of your choice, all the way up to the crimp. Bake the crust for about 30 minutes, or until the crimps are set. Remove from the oven and carefully lift out the foil and pie weights. Return the crust to the oven and bake for another 10 to 20 minutes, or until the crust is evenly browned. Remove and cool on a wire rack until ready to fill (no need to cool it completely).

(Continued)

VARIATIONS

Crumb Crust: For a quick and tasty alternative to the All-Butter Pie Crust, follow the directions for the Graham Cracker Crust (page 90). Either graham crackers or gingersnaps pair nicely with the pumpkin pie filling.

Maple: Replace the brown sugar with 160 grams (½ cup) of pure maple syrup, preferably dark amber.

Crème Fraîche: Replace the heavy cream with 168 grams (¾ cup) of crème fraîche.

BAKER'S NOTES

I like to blind-bake my pumpkin pie crusts because I prefer a crisp pastry, but you can skip this step if you don't mind a softer bottom crust. Make sure the crust is completely chilled before filling and baking.

PUMPKIN PIE *with* BUTTER PECAN STREUSEL (CONTINUED)

Make the Brown Butter Pecan Streusel: Lower the oven temperature to 325°F (160°C) and line a baking sheet with parchment paper or a silicone mat.

Place the butter in a small, light-colored saucepan over low-medium heat. Once the butter has melted, turn the heat up to medium-high. Stir frequently with a heatproof spatula, scraping the sides and bottom of the pan as needed. The butter will crackle, foam, turn clear gold, then finally start browning. It's done when the crackling subsides and you smell toasted nuts. This process takes about 10 minutes total, but the butter can go from browned to burnt in a flash—so keep an eye on it. Scrape the butter and all the toasty bits into a bowl and let cool to room temperature.

Whisk together the flour, sugars, salt, and pecans. Drizzle with the cooled browned butter, and stir until combined. Crumble with your fingertips until desired consistency is reached (I like pressing handfuls together to get some larger clumps). Spread the streusel on the prepared baking sheet and bake for 20 to 25 minutes, or until browned and no longer damp. Cool completely before using.

Assemble and Bake the Pumpkin Pie: Preheat the oven to 350°F (175°C) with a rack in the middle.

Whisk the cream, milk, eggs, vanilla, and bourbon (if using) together in a glass measuring cup. Combine the pumpkin puree, sugar, spices, and salt in a medium saucepan. Bring to a sputtering simmer over medium heat, stirring frequently with a heatproof spatula to avoid scorching. Continue to simmer the pumpkin mixture, stirring constantly, until thick and shiny, about 5 minutes.

Remove the pan from the heat and whisk in the cream mixture until fully incorporated. Strain the mixture into a medium bowl, using a spatula to press the solids through the strainer—this takes a little time and effort but ensures a silky-smooth texture. Re-whisk the mixture and scrape it into the prepared pie shell. Return the pie plate on a foil-lined baking sheet to the oven.

Bake the pie for 45 to 55 minutes, or until the edges of the pie are set but the very center still wobbles like set jello. Transfer the pie to a wire rack and cool for 15 minutes. Add the streusel topping to the pie and cool completely, about 3 hours. Pumpkin pie is best served the day it's baked. Refrigerate leftovers in an airtight container for up to 3 days.

CHICKEN POT PIE

MAKES ONE 9–INCH (23–CM)
DEEP–DISH PIE

CHICKEN FILLING
454 g (1 lb) skinless boneless chicken thighs, cut into ½-inch (1.25-cm) cubes

10 g (2½ tsp) kosher salt, plus more to taste

Olive oil, for the pan

1 large carrot, peeled and diced

2 celery stalks, diced

1 large onion, peeled and diced

4 cloves garlic, minced

1 bay leaf

2 g (2 tsp) thyme

Black pepper, to taste

1 kg (1 L) chicken stock

1 medium Yukon gold potato, peeled and diced

227 g (½ lb) cremini mushrooms, stemmed, cleaned, and quartered

70 g (5 tbsp) unsalted butter

75 g (½ cup plus 2 tbsp) all-purpose flour

125 g (1 cup) frozen corn or peas

½ tsp paprika

15 g (¼ cup) parsley, chopped

I'm married to a fellow foodie, which means that most long weekends you can find us tackling some kind of culinary project: ramen from scratch, homemade tofu, growing mushrooms, curing sausages, and so on. This chicken pot pie was one such project—he worked on the filling while I tackled the pastry. The result is a hearty, double-crusted pie that boasts a thick, flavorful filling and crisp, flaky crust. We like to use a deep-dish pie plate so that you can pack in plenty of filling. If you only have a standard pie plate, you can bake off the extras in mini pie plates for a baker's (and cook's!) treat.

Make the Chicken Filling: In a large bowl, combine the chicken and salt. Let rest for at least 30 minutes at room temperature (or up to 24 hours refrigerated).

Heat the oil over medium heat in a Dutch oven or large, heavy bottomed pot until glistening. Brown the chicken in batches, about 5 minutes per batch, and set aside.

In the same pot over medium heat, adding more oil if necessary, sauté the carrot, celery, onion, garlic, bay leaf, and thyme until the onion is translucent and the carrot and celery are softened, about 10 minutes. Season with salt and pepper to taste.

Add the chicken stock to pot to deglaze. Add the potato and mushrooms. Season with salt and pepper, to taste. Bring to a boil over medium-high heat, then lower heat and simmer, uncovered, until the liquid is reduced by one-third, about 30 minutes.

While the broth is reducing, make a roux by melting the butter over medium heat in a small saucepan. Once melted, immediately add all the flour, and whisk vigorously until combined. Turn the heat up to medium-high and continue cooking, whisking constantly, until the roux deepens in color, about 7 to 10 minutes. Remove from heat.

Once the stock has reduced, add about 480 grams (2 cups) of the stock to the saucepan with the roux. Whisk until smooth, then pour the roux-stock mixture into the pot along with the reserved chicken. Bring the mixture back to a simmer and cook until thickened, about 5 to 10 minutes, stirring frequently to avoid sticking.

Remove from the heat and stir in the corn, paprika, and parsley. Taste and adjust the seasoning as needed. Remove the bay leaf. Cool to room temperature before filling the pie. (The filling can be prepared and refrigerated in an airtight container for up to 3 days in advance or frozen for up to 3 months; defrost in the fridge the night before you plan to assemble and bake the pie).

(Continued)

1 batch All-Butter Pie Crust
(page 52)

TO FINISH
1 large egg, whisked with 1 tsp milk
or water and a pinch of salt, for egg
wash
Flaky salt, for garnishing

Assemble and Bake the Pie: Remove one disc of the chilled pie dough from the fridge and let it stand for about 5 to 10 minutes, just long enough to make it pliable. On a floured surface, roll into a 13-inch (33-cm) round just under ¼ inch (6 mm) thick. Roll from the center out, giving the dough a quarter turn after every roll to avoid sticking and ensure an even thickness. Dust off any excess flour. Carefully roll the dough onto the rolling pin and unfurl into a 9 x 2-inch (23 x 5-cm) deep-dish pie plate. Gently lift the edges and press the dough into the bottom and sides of the plate, being careful not to stretch the dough to fit. Trim the overhang to 1 inch (2.5 cm) all around. Remove the other disc of dough from the fridge and roll into a 13-inch (33-cm) round.

Spoon the cooled chicken filling evenly into the prepared pie plate, filling until just flush with the rim. (Do not mound. Depending on the size of your dish, you may have a little extra filling.) Brush the exposed rim of the pie dough with water, then center the second round of pie dough over the filling. Press the edges of the two crusts together, then trim the overhang to 1 inch (2.5 cm) all around. Tuck the overhang under itself and press onto the edges of the pie plate to seal. Crimp the border as desired. Chill the pie until the pastry is firm, about 30 to 60 minutes, while the oven preheats.

Preheat the oven to 400°F (200°C) with a rack in the lower third. If you have a baking steel or stone, preheat that as well. If not, preheat a large foil-lined baking sheet.

Right before baking, brush the crust with the egg wash and sprinkle with flaky salt. Cut several vent holes in the top crust for steam to escape. Bake for about 45 to 60 minutes, or until the crust is deeply golden and the filling is bubbling in the center. (Tent with foil partway through baking if the crust is browning too quickly.) Remove from the oven and cool for about 20 minutes before slicing. Chicken pot pie is best served the day it's baked. Refrigerate leftovers in an airtight container for up to 3 days.

VARIATIONS

Beef: Omit the paprika and parsley. Replace the chicken with 454 grams (1 lb) of stewing beef, cut into 1-inch (2.5-cm) chunks, and replace the chicken stock with the same volume of beef stock and/ or beer. Add the browned beef back to the pot with the potato and mushrooms, along with 15 grams (1 tbsp) of Dijon mustard and a couple of dashes of Worcestershire sauce. Bring to a boil, then cover and transfer to preheated 350°F (175°C) oven for about 1½ to 2 hours, or until the beef is tender.

Fish: Replace the chicken with 454 grams (1 lb) of firm white fish fillets such as pickerel, cod, or halibut, cut into 1-inch (2.5-cm) chunks. Season but do not brown the fish. Combine the raw fish pieces with the filling just before assembling the pie.

Puff Pastry Top: Instead of using a double pie crust, simply pour the filling (while still hot is fine) into a pie dish or similar-sized ovenproof vessel and drape 1 sheet of puff pastry—store-bought or ½ batch of the homemade Rough Puff Pastry (page 126)—slightly larger than the pie dish over the top. Brush the pastry with the egg wash and cut a couple of slits for ventilation. Place on a baking sheet and bake in a preheated 425°F (220°C) oven until the pastry is puffed and golden and the filling is bubbling, about 30 minutes.

MANGO & STRAWBERRY CREAM TART

MAKES ONE 9–INCH (23–CM)
TART

PÂTE SUCRÉE CRUST (MAKES ENOUGH FOR 2 TARTS)
250 g (2 cups) all-purpose flour
50 g (½ cup) almond flour
75 g (⅔ cup) icing sugar
½ tsp kosher salt
143 g (10 tbsp) unsalted butter, cold and cubed
1 large egg, cold
½ tsp pure vanilla extract

If you're looking for a simple, classy way to end a meal, you can't go wrong with a fresh fruit tart. I love the combination of crisp pastry, creamy filling, and glistening fresh fruit—a delight to the eyes and taste buds! This vibrant take on the classic dessert was inspired by my kids' favorites fruits—mangoes and strawberries.

Make the Pâte Sucrée Crust: Place the flours, icing sugar, and salt in the bowl of a food processor. Pulse a few times to combine. Scatter the butter over the top of the flour mixture. Pulse several times until the butter is about the size of peas.

Whisk together the egg and vanilla. Add the egg mixture in three stages, pulsing after each addition. Once all the egg is added, pulse in 10-second increments until the dough forms clumps but is not completely smooth. Once the dough reaches this stage, remove half of the dough and place on a piece of parchment.

Place a piece of plastic wrap on top of the dough. Use your hands to press the dough into a round, then roll it out into a roughly 12-inch (30-cm) circle about ¼ inch (6 mm) thick. Lift and replace the top piece of plastic occasionally to avoid creases in the dough. Slide the sheet of dough onto a baking sheet (still sandwiched between the parchment and plastic). Refrigerate until cold, at least 1 hour.

Repeat this process with the other half of the dough, or press it into a disc about ¾ inch (2 cm) thick, wrap tightly in plastic, and freeze for later use. Thaw overnight in the fridge before using.

Prepare the Tart Crust: Remove one of the unbaked crusts from the fridge and let it stand for about 5 to 10 minutes, just to make it pliable. Lightly grease a 9-inch (23-cm) tart tin. Turn the dough into the tart tin. Gently lift the edges and press the dough into the bottom and sides of the tin. Don't worry if it cracks or breaks here and there; the dough is forgiving and you can gently press it back together.

Trim the edge of the dough so it's even with the top of the tart tin (you can gently roll a rolling pin over the top or use a small paring knife). If there are any tears or cracks, use some of the extra dough to patch it up; reserve the extra dough for repairing any cracks that might appear after baking. Pierce the bottom of the dough all over with a fork, then wrap in plastic and freeze for at least 30 minutes.

Preheat the oven to 375°F (190°C) with a rack in the middle.

Remove the chilled tart tin from the freezer. Lightly grease the dull side of a piece of foil and fit it firmly over the chilled tart dough. Place the tart tin on a baking sheet and bake for 20 minutes. Remove the foil (if the crust has risen at all, press it down gently with the back of a spoon). If any cracks have formed, use some of the reserved dough to patch them. Bake the crust for another 5 to 10 minutes, or until firm and golden brown. Transfer to a wire rack and allow to cool completely before filling.

(Continued)

VARIATIONS

Pastry Cream Swaps: Use the recipe for Vanilla-Almond Pastry Cream (page 162), omitting the almond extract and increasing the vanilla to 10 grams (2 tsp). For chocolate pastry cream, stir 170 grams (1 cup) of finely chopped chocolate (whatever kind you prefer) into the vanilla pastry cream after the butter. For coconut pastry cream, follow the instructions for the vanilla pastry cream but replace 240 grams (1 cup) of whole milk with 240 grams (1 cup) of full-fat canned coconut milk. (Gelatin can be omitted with these variations, as the pastry cream is stiffer without the fruit puree.)

Fruit Topping Swaps: Replace or supplement the mangoes and strawberries with whatever fruit is fresh and in season. An assortment of berries is classic, but sliced kiwis, fresh figs, and stone fruit also work beautifully.

Crust Variations: For a chocolate crust, replace the almond flour with 22 grams (3 tbsp) of Dutch-processed cocoa powder. Increase the icing sugar to 100 grams (¾ cup plus 1 tbsp) and the butter to 175 grams (12½ tbsp). Or try this recipe with a Graham Cracker Crust (page 90) or Pretzel Tart Crust (page 72)!

BAKER'S NOTES

I like to use canned mango pulp, which is readily available at Asian supermarkets or online suppliers. You can make your own by blending and straining ripe mangoes, though you may wish to add a touch of extra sugar depending on the sweetness of your fruit.

MANGO PASTRY CREAM

390 g (1½ cups plus 2 tbsp) whole milk, divided

1 tsp pure vanilla extract

6 g (2 tsp) powdered gelatin

75 g (¼ cup plus 2 tbsp) granulated sugar, divided

¼ tsp kosher salt

26 g (3½ tbsp) cornstarch or custard powder

4 large egg yolks

28 g (2 tbsp) unsalted butter, cold and cubed

120 g (½ cup) mango pulp, preferably Alphonso (see Baker's Notes)

120 g (½ cup) heavy cream, cold

TO FINISH

Fresh strawberries and mangoes

80 g (¼ cup) apricot jam

Make the Mango Pastry Cream: Place a strainer over a large heat-safe bowl.

Place 30 grams (2 tbsp) of milk and the vanilla in a small bowl. Sprinkle the gelatin evenly over the top and allow to bloom while preparing the rest of the pastry cream.

Off heat, place the remaining 360 grams (1½ cups) of milk, 50 grams (¼ cup) of sugar, and the salt in a medium saucepan.

In a medium bowl, whisk together the remaining 25 grams (2 tbsp) of sugar and the cornstarch or custard powder. Pour in 1 tablespoon or so of the milk-sugar mixture and whisk until smooth. Add the egg yolks and whisk until smooth.

Heat the milk-sugar mixture over medium heat until steaming. Remove from the heat. Pour the milk in a slow, steady stream into the egg yolk mixture, whisking constantly. Scrape the custard mixture back into the saucepan and return to medium heat. Cook, whisking constantly, until the mixture thickens and large bubbles appear on the surface. Once the bubbles appear, turn down the heat to medium-low and continue whisking on the heat for 2 minutes.

Remove the custard from the heat and whisk in the bloomed gelatin. Once the gelatin has dissolved, whisk in the butter and the mango pulp.

Strain the pastry cream into the prepared container. Press a piece of plastic wrap against the surface of the pastry cream and cool to room temperature. (You can speed up the cooling process by placing the bowl over an ice bath and whisking occasionally, or by refrigerating. Just don't let it get too cold or the gelatin will start to set, making it difficult to incorporate the whipped cream.)

Assemble and Decorate the Tart: Once the pastry cream has cooled, whip the heavy cream to medium peaks. Whisk the pastry cream to loosen, then use a flexible spatula to gently fold the whipped cream into the pastry cream in three additions.

Fill the tart shell with the pastry cream, spreading it out smoothly with a small offset spatula. Refrigerate until set, at least 1 hour.

Once the tart is set (and as close to serving as possible), arrange the fresh strawberries and mangoes on top as desired. In a microwave or in a small saucepan on the stove, gently warm the apricot jam. Strain, then brush the jam generously over the top of the fruit. If not serving immediately, refrigerate until ready to serve. The tart is best served the day it is made, when the pastry is still crisp.

BOURBON BUTTER TARTS

MAKES 12 TARTS

BUTTER TART CRUST
250 g (2 cups) all-purpose flour

125 g (1 cup) whole-grain flour (such as whole-wheat, spelt, kamut, or rye)

6 g (1½ tsp) kosher salt

13 g (1 tbsp) granulated sugar

250 g (1 cup plus 2 tbsp) unsalted butter, cold and cut into ½-inch (1.25-cm) cubes

1 large egg yolk

15 g (1 tbsp) vinegar or lemon juice

80 g (⅓ cup) ice water, divided, more or less as needed

The butter tart is perhaps Canada's most iconic dessert, beloved across the nation. It consists of flaky pastry filled with a sweet, caramelly filling often compared to the innards of a chess or pecan pie (sans pecans). What makes a perfect butter tart is a point of continual debate—with runny vs. firm filling and raisins vs. no raisins being the hottest points of contention. (I'm in the firm filling, no raisins camp.) Butter tarts can teeter on the edge of cloyingly sweet, so I've taken a few measures to keep things in balance—namely whole-grain flour in the crust and brown butter and bourbon in the filling. As for the raisins? Well, I'll leave that up to you.

Make the Butter Tart Crust: In a large bowl, whisk together the flours, salt, and sugar. Scatter the butter over the top. Use the pads of your fingers to flatten the butter pieces, tossing them with the flour mixture so each piece is coated on all sides. The butter pieces should remain fairly large, about the size of walnuts. Work quickly so the butter remains cold.

In a small bowl, whisk together the egg yolk, vinegar, and 30 grams (2 tbsp) of the ice water. Drizzle the liquid over the flour-butter mixture and use a fork or your hands to "toss" the two together, similar to the way you would dress salad greens. Add additional water, 1 or 2 teaspoons at a time, tossing after each addition, until the dough just holds together when you squeeze a bit in your hand. (I usually need an additional 50 grams [3 tbsp] or so, but the amount can vary depending on the flour you're using and the humidity.) Fold the dough over itself several times, giving the bowl a quarter turn after each fold, to make a cohesive but ragged mass. You should still see visible pieces of butter—this is a good thing! Transfer the dough to a piece of plastic wrap and pat into a rectangle. Wrap to seal, then use your hands or a rolling pin to flatten the dough to about ¾ inch (2 cm) thick. Refrigerate for 30 minutes.

Transfer the chilled dough to a lightly floured surface. Using a floured rolling pin, roll the dough into a roughly 13-inch (33-cm) square. Brush off any extra flour and fold the dough into thirds like a letter. Fold into thirds again so you end up with a roughly 4½-inch (11-cm) square. Roll into a ¾-inch (2-cm)-thick rectangle twice as long as it is wide and cut in half. Wrap and refrigerate one half.

Transfer the other half to a lightly floured piece of parchment and roll the dough into a rectangle about 9½ x 14 inches (24 x 36 cm), just under ¼ inch (6 mm) thick. Slide the dough, still on the parchment, onto a baking sheet. Repeat with the second piece of dough. Slide the second piece, still on the parchment, on top of the first. Cover and refrigerate for 1 hour.

(Continued)

BUTTER TART FILLING

57 g (¼ cup) unsalted butter
150 g (¾ cup) light brown sugar
½ tsp kosher salt
2 large eggs, straight from the fridge
80 g (¼ cup) light corn syrup or golden syrup
15 g (1 tbsp) bourbon
1 tsp pure vanilla extract
10 g (2 tsp) vinegar
12 g (1½ tbsp) all-purpose flour

Fill, Assemble, and Bake the Tarts: Preheat the oven to 425°F (220°C) with a rack in the lower third. Have ready a standard ungreased 12-cup muffin tin.

Remove one sheet of dough from the fridge. Use a round cookie cutter to punch out six 4½-inch (11-cm) circles. Ease each round gently into a muffin cup, pinching the edges inward every 90 degrees to form a four-leaf clover shape. The edges of the pastry should meet or slightly extend the top of the muffin cups. Repeat with the second piece of dough. Freeze while you prepare the filling. (Dough scraps can be refrigerated or frozen for another recipe.)

To prepare the filling, cube the butter and place in a small, light-colored saucepan over low-medium heat. Once the butter has melted, turn the heat up to medium-high. Stir frequently with a heatproof spatula, scraping the sides and bottom of the pan as needed. The butter will crackle, foam, turn clear gold, then finally start browning. It's done when the crackling subsides and you smell toasted nuts. This process takes about 10 minutes total, but the butter can go from browned to burnt in a flash—so keep an eye on it.

Remove the browned butter from the heat and scrape it and all the toasty bits into a large bowl. Cool for about 5 minutes, then whisk in the brown sugar and salt (it might not be completely smooth, but that's fine). Whisk in the eggs one at a time, followed by the corn syrup, bourbon, vanilla, vinegar, and flour.

Divide the filling evenly among the tart shells, about 32 grams (2 tbsp) each, leaving about ½-inch (1.25-cm) headspace. Place the muffin tin on a baking sheet and transfer to the preheated oven. Bake for about 15 to 20 minutes, or until the pastry is golden and the tops are puffed and set.

Cool the tarts in the pan, then use an offset spatula or knife to carefully remove the tarts and transfer to a wire rack to cool completely. Serve at room temperature. Store leftovers in an airtight container for up to 5 days.

VARIATIONS

Maple-Pecan: Replace the corn or golden syrup with 80 grams (¼ cup) of pure maple syrup. Divide 60 grams (½ cup) of toasted, chopped pecans among the muffin tins before pouring in the filling mixture.

Rum-Raisin: Replace the bourbon with dark rum. Divide 75 grams (½ cup) of raisins among the muffin tins before pouring in the filling mixture.

Butter Tart Squares: Make half a batch of the vanilla variation of Matcha Shortbread (pages 40–41) and press evenly into a foil or parchment-lined and lightly greased 8 x 8-inch (20 x 20–cm) pan. Prick the surface all over with a fork and bake in a preheated 350°F (175°C) oven for 15 minutes, or until set. Keep the oven on, and cool the crust on a wire rack while making the filling. Prepare the filling as directed, then pour over the pre-baked crust. Bake for about 25 minutes, or until the filling is set in the center. Cool completely before cutting into squares (for the cleanest slices, chill before cutting).

CHOCOLATE CARAMEL PRETZEL TART

MAKES ONE 9-INCH (23-CM) TART

PRETZEL TART CRUST (MAKES 1 CRUST)
125 g (1 cup) salted pretzel crumbs (from about 3 cups mini pretzels)
100 g (1 cup) graham cracker crumbs
39 g (3 tbsp) light brown sugar
Pinch of kosher salt
98 g (7 tbsp) unsalted butter, melted and cooled
1 large egg white, lightly whisked

CARAMEL LAYER
100 g (½ cup) granulated sugar
30 g (1½ tbsp) light corn syrup
22 g (1½ tbsp) water
45 g (3 tbsp) heavy cream, warm
42 g (3 tbsp) unsalted butter, at room temperature and cubed
¼ tsp fine sea salt

CHOCOLATE GANACHE
140 g (¾ cup) milk chocolate, finely chopped (35–45% cacao)
140 g (¾ cup) dark chocolate, finely chopped (60–70% cacao)
28 g (2 tbsp) unsalted butter, at room temperature and cubed
200 g (¾ cup plus 4 tsp) heavy cream
20 g (1 tbsp) light corn syrup
Pinch of kosher salt
1 tsp pure vanilla extract

TO FINISH
Mini pretzels
Flaky sea salt
Salted Caramel Sauce (page 164) (optional)

A chocolate tart is the little black dress of desserts—simple, elegant, and always in style. This version is inspired by some pretzel caramel chocolates that were served at our wedding. My husband and I didn't get to eat any during the reception, so we got a box to go. I managed to eat them all and have never quite lived that down, so now every anniversary I try to make a treat using those same delicious flavors—and do my best to share. The chocolate is really the star in this tart, so use the best quality you can.

Make the Pretzel Tart Crust: Preheat the oven to 350°F (175°C) with a rack in the middle.

In a medium bowl, mix together the pretzel crumbs, graham cracker crumbs, sugar, salt, butter, and egg white together. Press the mixture firmly and evenly into the bottom and up the sides of a 9-inch (23-cm) tart pan. I like to use a small measuring cup or shot glass to compact the crumbs into the pan.

Bake the crust for about 10 minutes, or until set. Cool completely on a wire rack before filling.

Make the Caramel Layer: In a medium saucepan, combine the sugar, corn syrup, and water. Stir with a fork until all the sugar is evenly moistened. Cook over medium heat, stirring occasionally, until the sugar is dissolved.

Once the mixture begins bubbling, stop stirring. Let the mixture boil undisturbed until it turns the color of an old copper penny. Immediately remove from the heat and carefully pour in the warm cream, stirring constantly, until smooth. Add the butter and salt and stir until completely combined, being sure to scrape the bottom of the pan. Return to low heat and cook for about 30 to 60 seconds to slightly thicken the caramel, stirring constantly.

Pour the caramel into the prepared tart crust and quickly tilt the pan to cover the entire bottom. Cool to room temperature, then refrigerate while you prepare the ganache.

Make the Chocolate Ganache: Place the chopped chocolate and butter in a heat-safe bowl. In a medium saucepan, heat the cream, corn syrup, and salt just until steaming. Remove from the heat, pour over the chocolate, and let stand for 3 minutes. Gently whisk to form a smooth, shiny ganache. Add the vanilla and whisk until combined. Pour the ganache over the caramel layer. Allow to set completely at room temperature, about 2 hours (you can speed this along in the fridge, but bring to room temperature about 30 minutes before serving).

Finish the Tart: Right before serving, garnish the tart with the mini pretzels and a sprinkle of flaky salt. Serve with an extra drizzle of Salted Caramel Sauce (page 164), if desired. The tart is best served the day it is made. Refrigerate leftovers in an airtight container for up to 5 days.

VARIATIONS

Classic Chocolate Ganache Tart: Replace the pretzel crust with either a classic or chocolate Pâte Sucrée Crust (page 66). Omit the caramel layer. Garnish with flaky salt or fresh fruit.

Earl Grey Ganache: When making the ganache, add 10 grams (2 tbsp) of loose-leaf Earl Grey tea to the cream mixture. Once steaming, remove from the heat, cover, and let steep for 10 minutes. Reheat again to steaming, then strain over the chopped chocolate. This variation pairs well with a classic or chocolate Pâte Sucrée Crust (page 66) in place of the pretzel crust. Garnish with flaky salt.

Peanut: When making the ganache, reduce the butter to 1 teaspoon and add 32 grams (2 tbsp) of smooth peanut butter. Garnish with chopped salted, roasted peanuts, and flaky salt.

FOR ANY OCCASION: CAKES

Whether it's a birthday, wedding, or simple gathering with friends, cake is always welcome!

One of the ways I fell in love with baking was by making birthday cakes for all my friends. It was a perfect creative outlet for testing new recipes, flavor combinations, and decorating ideas (thanks for being my guinea pigs, guys!); but more importantly, it reminded me time and again that the best part of baking is being able to share your creations and bring joy to others.

Baking for a potluck? Try the Carrot Cake for a Crowd (page 82) or Earl Grey Bundt Cake (page 84). Mom's Sponge Cake (page 92) or the Strawberry-Elderflower Fraisier (page 87) are perfect light endings for a summer dinner with friends—or break out the decadent David's Chocolate-Raspberry Cake (page 76) for a special celebration.

The variations for each recipe offer further options for personalizing these cakes through alternate fillings and frostings, flavor tweaks, and size adaptations. The recipes in this chapter are my favorites for celebrating the special moments in life. I hope they'll bring smiles and a little magic to you and yours, too.

DAVID'S CHOCOLATE–RASPBERRY CAKE

MAKES ONE 6–INCH (15–CM) THREE–LAYER CAKE

QUICK RASPBERRY JAM
400 g (3¼ cups) fresh or frozen raspberries

100 g (½ cup) granulated sugar

Squeeze of lemon juice

CHOCOLATE CAKE
68 g (½ cup plus 1 tbsp) Dutch-processed cocoa powder, plus more to dust the pans

113 g (½ cup) unsalted butter, cubed

55 g (¼ cup) neutral vegetable oil, such as grapeseed or canola

120 g (½ cup) whole milk

10 g (2 tsp) pure vanilla extract

250 g (2 cups) all-purpose flour

330 g (1⅔ cups) light brown sugar

1 tsp kosher salt

7 g (1½ tsp) baking soda

160 g (⅔ cup) sour cream, at room temperature

2 large eggs, at room temperature

120 g (½ cup) freshly brewed hot coffee

SILKY FUDGE FROSTING
340 g (1½ cups) unsalted butter, at room temperature

120 g (1 cup) icing sugar

60 g (½ cup) Dutch-processed cocoa powder

80 g (⅓ cup) hot water

80 g (⅓ cup) sour cream

1 tsp pure vanilla extract

½ tsp kosher salt

200 g (1 cup plus 2 tbsp) good quality dark chocolate (60–70% cacao), melted and cooled

My husband is generally an adventurous eater; but when it comes to dessert, he's a creature of habit. I've stopped asking him what kind of cake he wants for his birthday—the answer is, and always will be, chocolate-raspberry. This is my go-to rendition: a rich chocolate cake layered with both raspberry jam and fresh raspberries, all covered in a silky-smooth chocolate fudge frosting.

Make the Quick Raspberry Jam: Combine the raspberries, sugar, and lemon juice in a medium saucepan and bring to a boil over medium heat, stirring and smashing the berries occasionally with a heatproof spatula. Once the mixture reaches a boil, continue cooking for about 10 to 15 minutes, stirring frequently, until thick and viscous. Strain the jam into a heatproof container to remove the seeds and cool to room temperature. Refrigerate the jam until ready to use.

Make the Chocolate Cake Layers: Preheat the oven to 350°F (175°C) with a rack in the middle. Grease three 6-inch (15-cm) round cake pans and line the bottoms with parchment paper, then grease the pans again and dust them with the cocoa powder.

In a small saucepan, melt the butter over low heat. When the butter has melted, remove from the heat, and whisk in the oil, milk, and vanilla. Allow to cool slightly while you prepare the rest of the ingredients.

Sift together the flour, cocoa powder, sugar, salt, and baking soda in a large bowl. Set aside.

Whisk the sour cream into the butter mixture, followed by the eggs. Whisk the wet ingredients into the dry until combined. Add the hot coffee and whisk just until smooth.

Divide the batter equally among the prepared pans, about 430 grams each, and bake for 30 to 35 minutes or until a skewer inserted into the center comes out with just a few moist crumbs. Transfer to a wire rack to cool. Once the pans are cool enough to handle, run an offset spatula around the edges and turn the cakes out to finish cooling completely. For easiest assembly, wrap each layer in plastic wrap and chill in the fridge until firm before filling and frosting, at least 2 hours or up to 3 days.

Make the Silky Fudge Frosting: Combine the butter, icing sugar, cocoa powder, hot water, sour cream, vanilla, and salt in the bowl of a food processor. Pulse until well combined. Add the melted chocolate and pulse until smooth.

(Continued)

VARIATIONS

Cupcakes: The chocolate cake recipe makes about 24 regular cupcakes. Fill liners about halfway full and bake at 350°F (175°C) for 18 to 20 minutes. If you want to add raspberry filling, use a paring knife or apple corer to remove a piece from the center of each cupcake.

Bundt Cake: The chocolate cake recipe makes one large (10- to 12-cup) Bundt cake. Grease and dust the pan with the cocoa powder before filling and bake at 350°F (175°C) for 35 to 45 minutes, or until a skewer inserted in the center comes out clean. Finish with a Sour Cream Glaze (page 140), White Chocolate Glaze (page 156), Salted Caramel Sauce (page 164), or a simple dusting of icing sugar.

Chocolate Stout Cake: Omit the milk and coffee. Add 240 grams (1 cup) of stout beer (such as Guinness) to the melted butter with the oil and vanilla. Add 4 grams (2 tsp) of espresso powder to the dry ingredients.

Alternative Frostings: This cake also pairs well with Vanilla Swiss Meringue Buttercream (page 79) or Caramelized White Chocolate Cream Cheese Buttercream (page 82).

BAKER'S NOTES

I like the drama of a 6-inch (15-cm) cake, but you can also bake the chocolate cake in two 8-inch (20-cm) pans (start checking for doneness around 23 minutes).

The silky fudge frosting is adapted from Rosie Alyea of sweetapolita.com.

The recipe for the Quick Raspberry Jam makes more than you will need for filling the cake. Drizzle leftovers on the cake slices when serving, or freeze in an airtight container for up to 6 months.

Cakes   77

DAVID'S CHOCOLATE–RASPBERRY CAKE
(CONTINUED)

TO FINISH
125 g (1 cup) fresh raspberries, halved if large, plus more for decorating

Assemble the Cake: Trim the tops of the cake layers to level if needed and peel the parchment paper off each one. Fill a piping bag fitted with a plain round tip with about 1 cup of Silky Fudge Frosting.

Place a dollop of frosting on a cake board, plate, or cake stand and place the first cake round on top.

Spoon about ⅓ cup of frosting onto the first cake round and spread it on evenly using a small offset spatula. Pipe a ring of frosting around the edge of the cake to create a dam. Fill the center with an even layer of raspberry jam and press in a handful of the fresh raspberries.

Repeat with the second layer. Finish by placing on the last cake round, top side down (this keeps the crumbs in while also ensuring a flat top).

Use an offset spatula to spread a thin layer of frosting over the entire cake to lock the crumbs in. Refrigerate for about 15 minutes, or until the frosting is firm.

Spread on the remaining frosting and decorate as desired. Serve at room temperature. Refrigerate leftovers in an airtight container for up to 3 days.

ALMOND–BUTTERMILK LAYER CAKE

MAKES ONE 6–INCH (15–CM) THREE–LAYER CAKE

ALMOND–BUTTERMILK CAKE
250 g (2 cups) all-purpose flour

50 g (½ cup) almond flour

125 g (9 tbsp) unsalted butter, at room temperature

300 g (1½ cups) granulated sugar

10 g (2¼ tsp) baking powder

5 g (1¼ tsp) kosher salt

45 g (3 tbsp) neutral vegetable oil, such as grapeseed or canola

3 large eggs, at room temperature

15 g (1 tbsp) pure vanilla extract

¾ tsp pure almond extract

285 g (1 cup plus 3 tbsp) buttermilk, at room temperature

MEYER LEMON CURD
2 large eggs

2 large egg yolks

Pinch of salt

65 g (⅓ cup) granulated sugar

Zest of 2 Meyer lemons

125 g (½ cup) Meyer lemon juice, freshly squeezed

85 g (6 tbsp) unsalted butter, cubed

VANILLA SWISS MERINGUE BUTTERCREAM
120 g (½ cup) egg whites (from about 4 large eggs)

200 g (1 cup) granulated sugar

½ tsp kosher salt

⅛ tsp cream of tartar

395 g (1¾ cups) unsalted butter, at room temperature

8 g (1½ tsp) pure vanilla extract

Every baker needs a few go-to yellow cakes. I'm fond of this almond-buttermilk number because it's simple enough for everyday celebrations but also boasts a sophisticated flavor appropriate for more swanky affairs. A small amount of almond flour adds richness, and buttermilk ensures a tender crumb. This cake plays well with any number of fillings and frostings, but here I've added a slick of zesty Meyer lemon curd between the layers and covered it all in my go-to silky-smooth Vanilla Swiss Meringue Buttercream.

Make the Almond-Buttermilk Cake Layers: Preheat the oven to 350°F (175°C) with a rack in the middle. Line the bottoms of three 6-inch (15-cm) round cake pans with parchment paper, then grease the pans and dust them with flour.

In a small bowl, whisk the flour and almond flour together thoroughly.

In the bowl of a stand mixer fitted with the paddle attachment, combine the butter, sugar, baking powder, and salt. Mix on low to combine, then increase the speed to medium and cream until light and fluffy, about 5 minutes. Use a flexible spatula to scrape down the sides of the bowl and the paddle a couple of times during this process. Add the oil and mix well to combine. Scrape down the bowl and the paddle.

Add the eggs one at a time, making sure each is well incorporated before adding the next. Add the vanilla and almond extracts and mix well to combine. Scrape down the bowl and the paddle.

With the mixer on low, add the flour and buttermilk in five additions, beginning and ending with the flour. Use a flexible spatula to fold from the bottom of the bowl a few times to make sure the batter is well mixed. The mixture may look slightly curdled; this is normal for this batter due to the addition of almond flour.

Divide the batter equally among the prepared cake pans, about 385 grams each. Use an offset spatula to smooth the tops.

Bake until the cakes are puffed and lightly golden and a skewer inserted into the center comes out clean or with a few moist crumbs, about 25 to 32 minutes. Transfer to a wire rack to cool. Once the pans are cool enough to handle, run an offset spatula around the edges and turn the cakes out to finish cooling completely. For easiest assembly, wrap each layer in plastic wrap and chill in the fridge until firm before filling and frosting, at least 2 hours or up to 3 days.

(Continued)

ALMOND–BUTTERMILK LAYER CAKE (CONTINUED)

Make the Meyer Lemon Curd: Place a strainer over a heatproof container and set aside.

In a medium nonreactive saucepan, whisk together the eggs, yolks, salt, sugar, lemon zest, and lemon juice until well blended.

Add the butter cubes. Cook over low heat, stirring constantly, until the butter is melted.

Increase the heat slightly to medium-low and continue cooking and stirring constantly until the curd thickens and coats the back of a spoon, about 5 minutes (see Baker's Notes). Do not boil.

Immediately remove from the heat and press the curd through the strainer. Cool to room temperature, then cover and refrigerate until ready to use. The curd will thicken after chilling.

Make the Vanilla Swiss Meringue Buttercream: Fill a saucepan with about 3 inches (7.5 cm) of water and bring it to a simmer. Combine the egg whites, sugar, salt, and cream of tartar in the bowl of a stand mixer and whisk to combine. Place the bowl on top of the saucepan to create a double-boiler—this heats the egg mixture gently to avoid cooking the eggs. The base of the bowl should not touch the simmering water.

Heat the egg white mixture, stirring frequently and scraping the sides and bottom of the bowl with a heatproof spatula, until it reaches 165 to 170°F (74 to 77°C) on an instant-read thermometer. The mixture should be quite thick and foamy and the sugar completely dissolved.

Remove the bowl from the double-boiler and transfer to a stand mixer fitted with the whisk attachment. Whisk on medium-high for about 10 minutes, or until the meringue is shiny and holds medium-stiff peaks and the bowl has cooled to room temperature.

Turn the speed down to medium and add the butter about 2 tablespoons at a time. Once all the butter has been added, add the vanilla. Continue mixing until the buttercream is silky and smooth.

Assemble the Cake: Trim the tops of the cakes to level if needed and peel the parchment paper off each one. Fill a piping bag fitted with a plain round tip with about 1 cup of buttercream.

Place a dollop of frosting on a cake board, plate, or cake stand and place the first cake round on top.

Spoon about ⅓ cup of buttercream onto the first cake round and spread it on smoothly using a small offset spatula. Pipe a ring of buttercream around the edge of the cake to create a dam. Fill the center with an even layer of Meyer Lemon Curd.

Repeat with the second layer. Finish by placing on the last cake round, top side down (this keeps the crumbs in while also ensuring a flat top).

Use an offset spatula to spread a thin layer of buttercream over the entire cake to lock the crumbs in. Refrigerate for about 10 minutes, until set.

After the cake has chilled, frost and decorate as desired. Serve at room temperature. Refrigerate leftovers in an airtight container for up to 3 days.

VARIATIONS

Nut-Free Cake: Omit the almond flour. Decrease the all-purpose flour to 156 grams (1¼ cups) and add 156 grams (1¼ cups) of cake flour, sifted.

Filling Options: In the curd, replace the Meyer lemon juice and zest with lime juice and zest or regular lemon juice and zest. If using regular lemon juice, increase the sugar to 100 grams (½ cup). Fruit jam, such as Quick Raspberry Jam (page 76), also pairs well with this cake.

Birthday Cake: Omit the Meyer Lemon Curd. Fill and frost the cake with Silky Fudge Frosting (page 76), and decorate with sprinkles.

BAKER'S NOTES

It's important to remove the lemon curd from the heat right when it thickens or it may taste grainy after cooling. If you do end up with a grainy curd, you can restore the smooth texture by blending it briefly. The curd recipe makes more than you will need for this cake. You can freeze the leftovers for up to 1 year in an airtight container, or simply enjoy on toast or scones!

CARROT CAKE FOR A CROWD

MAKES ONE
9 X 13–INCH
(23 X 33–CM)
SHEET CAKE

I've tried a lot of carrot cake recipes over the years and pulled all my favorite elements together to create this version, which is well spiced and moist and studded with both nuts and raisins. And of course, cream cheese frosting is a given!

CARROT CAKE

170 g (¾ cup) unsalted butter, cubed

55 g (¼ cup) neutral vegetable oil, such as grapeseed or canola

60 g (¼ cup) buttermilk

3 large eggs, cold

150 g (¾ cup) granulated sugar

110 g (½ cup plus 2 tsp) light brown sugar

1 tsp kosher salt

7 g (1½ tsp) baking powder

½ tsp baking soda

5 g (2 tsp) ground cinnamon

3 g (2 tsp) ground ginger

¼ tsp freshly grated nutmeg

¼ tsp allspice

8 g (1½ tsp) pure vanilla extract

125 g (1 cup) all-purpose flour

125 g (1 cup) whole-wheat flour

340 g (3 cups) finely shredded carrots

100 g (¾ cup) toasted pecans or walnuts, finely chopped

75 g (½ cup) raisins, soaked in hot water for 20 minutes and drained (optional)

CARAMELIZED WHITE CHOCOLATE CREAM CHEESE BUTTERCREAM

188 g (1 cup plus 1 tbsp) good-quality blond chocolate (such as Valrhona Dulcey), finely chopped

250 g (1 block) cream cheese, at room temperature

125 g (½ cup plus 1 tbsp) unsalted butter, at room temperature

Pinch of salt, to taste

Make the Carrot Cake: Preheat the oven to 350°F (175°C) with a rack in the middle. Lightly grease and line a 9 x 13-inch (23 x 33-cm) cake pan with parchment paper that overhangs on the two long edges by at least 2 inches (5 cm). This will make it easy to remove the cake from the pan later. Lightly grease the parchment. Set aside.

To brown the butter, place the cubed butter in a small, light-colored saucepan over low-medium heat. Once the butter has melted, turn the heat up to medium-high. Stir frequently with a heatproof spatula, scraping the sides and bottom of the pan as needed. The butter will crackle, foam, turn clear gold, then finally start browning. It's done when the crackling subsides and you smell toasted nuts. This process takes about 10 minutes total, but the butter can go from browned to burnt in a flash—so keep an eye on it. Pour the butter and all the toasty bits into a glass measuring cup. Whisk in the oil and buttermilk and set aside.

In the bowl of a stand mixer fitted with the whisk attachment, combine the eggs, sugars, salt, baking powder, baking soda, cinnamon, ginger, nutmeg, allspice, and vanilla. Mix on low speed to combine, then turn up the speed to medium-high and whip until the mixture is thick and fluffy and roughly tripled in volume, 6 to 8 minutes. Meanwhile, whisk together the flours in a small bowl.

Turn down the mixer to low and slowly drizzle in the brown butter–oil–buttermilk mixture. Once the liquid is incorporated, add the flours. Once smooth, turn the mixer off and fold in the carrots, nuts, and raisins with a flexible spatula, mixing just until everything is evenly combined.

Scrape the batter into the prepared pan and smooth the top with an offset spatula. Bake until puffed and golden brown and a toothpick inserted in the center comes out clean, about 30 to 40 minutes. Cool on a wire rack completely before frosting.

Make the Caramelized White Chocolate Cream Cheese Buttercream: Place the chocolate in a heat-safe bowl. Microwave in 15-second increments, stirring well after each burst. When the chocolate is almost completely melted, allow the residual heat to complete the melting. Cool to room temperature.

In the bowl of a stand mixer fitted with the paddle attachment, combine the cream cheese and butter. Beat on medium-low until smooth and creamy. Do not overbeat. Gradually beat in the cooled, melted chocolate. Taste and add a pinch of salt if desired. Use immediately.

Assemble the Cake: Carefully transfer the cooled cake to a serving platter, using the excess parchment to lift it out, or leave it in the pan for easy transporting. Dollop the buttercream over the surface and use the back of a spoon or a small offset spatula to spread it over the top. Decorate as desired. Serve at room temperature. Refrigerate leftovers in an airtight container for up to 3 days.

Baked to Order

VARIATIONS

Coconut: Add 95 grams (1 cup) of shredded, dried coconut (sweetened or unsweetened) along with the shredded carrots. Use melted coconut oil for the oil (unrefined/virgin will add more coconut flavor). Garnish with lightly toasted coconut shreds or flakes.

Layer Cake: Prepare the batter as described and divide among three greased and parchment-lined 6-inch (15-cm) round cake pans. Bake at 350°F (175°C) for about 30 minutes, using the same visual cues to determine doneness. (The frosting amount is enough for a light coat; make one-and-a-half to two times the amount for full coverage.)

Cupcakes: Prepare the batter as described and fill cupcake liners about three-quarters full. Bake at 350°F (175°C) for about 18 to 22 minutes. Makes about 24 cupcakes. Make one-and-a-half to two times the amount of frosting.

BAKER'S NOTES

If you can't find blond chocolate, you can substitute an equal amount of plain, good quality white chocolate (at least 30 percent cocoa butter) instead. Alternatively, you can make your own blond or caramelized white chocolate. Coarsely chop about 340 grams (2 cups) of good quality white chocolate, spread it out on a baking sheet, and bake at 250°F (121°C), stirring every 10 minutes, until deeply golden and caramelized, about 40 to 60 minutes. Cool, then chop and store in an airtight jar at room temperature until ready to use.

EARL GREY BUNDT CAKE

MAKES ONE 12-CUP
BUNDT CAKE

EARL GREY–INFUSED BUTTER

280 g (1¼ cups) unsalted butter

30 g (6 tbsp) loose leaf Earl Grey tea

EARL GREY BUNDT CAKE

4 large eggs, at room temperature

10 g (2 tsp) pure vanilla extract

240 g (1 cup) sour cream, at room temperature, divided

156 g (1¼ cups) all-purpose flour

182 g (1½ cups minus 1 tsp) cake flour

8 g (2 tsp) baking powder

¼ tsp baking soda

5 g (1¼ tsp) kosher salt

350 g (1¾ cups) granulated sugar

175 g (¾ cup) Earl Grey–Infused Butter, at room temperature

55 g (¼ cup) neutral vegetable oil, such as grapeseed or canola

The most important cake I've baked to date was for my brother Tim and his now-wife Kelsey's wedding. They gave me full reign over the design, just requesting that Earl Grey be one of the flavors. This is a Bundt version of the cake I ended up creating for them. It begins with Earl Grey–infused butter, a simple but effective way to flavor baked goods with tea. The baked cake also gets brushed with an Earl Grey syrup and finished with a light lemon glaze. If you can, make this cake the day before you want to serve it to give the flavors time to meld and intensify.

Make the Earl Grey–Infused Butter: In a small saucepan over low heat, melt the butter until it liquefies. Add the tea leaves. Keep the pan on low heat for about 5 minutes, stirring occasionally.

Remove the pan from the heat and cover. Let stand for 15 to 30 minutes to allow the tea flavor to intensify.

Place a sieve over a bowl or glass measuring cup and pour in the butter mixture. Press on the tea leaves with the back of a spoon or spatula to extract as much liquid as possible. Discard the tea leaves.

Refrigerate the butter for about 30 minutes, or until it's the consistency of softened butter. Measure out 175 grams (12½ tbsp) of the infused butter for the cake; the remainder can be used on bread, scones, waffles, and such.

Make the Earl Grey Bundt Cake: Preheat the oven to 350°F (175°C) with a rack in the lower middle position. Generously grease and flour a 12-cup Bundt pan.

In a glass measuring cup with a spout, whisk together the eggs, vanilla, and 60 grams (¼ cup) of the sour cream.

In the bowl of a stand mixer fitted with a paddle attachment, combine the flours, baking powder, baking soda, salt, and sugar. Mix on low for 30 seconds to combine.

With the mixer still on low, add the Earl Grey–Infused Butter a spoonful at a time, followed by the oil and the remaining 180 grams (¾ cup) of sour cream. Once all the flour is moistened, increase the speed to medium and beat for about 90 seconds. The batter will be very thick at this point. Scrape down the sides of the bowl and paddle.

With the mixer on low, add half of the egg and sour cream mixture. Increase the speed to medium and beat for 30 seconds. Scrape down the sides of the bowl and paddle. Repeat with the remaining egg mixture.

Fold the batter a couple of times with a flexible spatula to ensure everything is well incorporated. Scrape the batter into the prepared Bundt pan and smooth the surface with a small offset spatula.

(Continued)

VARIATIONS

Vanilla: Replace the infused butter with regular unsalted room temperature butter and increase the vanilla to 20 grams (4 tsp). Omit the Earl Grey tea from the simple syrup. Replace the lemon juice in the glaze with additional milk or cream.

Cardamom: Replace the infused butter with regular unsalted room temperature butter and add 6 grams (1½ tsp) of freshly ground cardamom to the flour-sugar mixture. Omit the Earl Grey tea from the simple syrup. Replace the lemon juice in the glaze with additional milk or cream.

Alternative Sizes: This cake can be baked in four 6-inch (15-cm) round cake pans, two 9-inch (23-cm) round cake pans, or two 8½ x 4½-inch (22 x 11-cm) or 9 x 5-inch (23 x 13-cm) loaf pans. For round cake layers, start checking for doneness around 25 minutes; for loaves, around 45 minutes. For layer cakes, I like pairing with Meyer Lemon Curd (page 79) and frosting with either Vanilla Swiss Meringue Buttercream (page 79) or Caramelized White Chocolate Cream Cheese Buttercream (page 82).

BAKER'S NOTES

To check the volume of your Bundt pan, use a liquid measuring cup to fill the pan completely with water. Keep track of how many cups—this is the size of your pan. If your Bundt pan is smaller than 12 cups, fill it no more than two-thirds full of batter. Bake off the leftover batter as cupcakes or mini loaves.

EARL GREY SIMPLE SYRUP
65 g (⅓ cup) granulated sugar
80 g (⅓ cup) water
3 g (2 tsp) loose leaf Earl Grey tea

LEMON GLAZE
120 g (1 cup) icing sugar
Pinch of kosher salt
1 tsp unsalted butter, melted
15 g (1 tbsp) milk
15 g (1 tbsp) freshly squeezed
lemon juice, plus more as needed

Place the Bundt pan on a baking sheet and bake for 45 to 60 minutes, or until a skewer inserted near the center comes out clean and the cake is springy to the touch.

Prepare the Earl Grey Simple Syrup: While the cake is baking, bring the sugar and water to a boil over medium-high heat in a small saucepan. Reduce the heat to low and bring the mixture down to a simmer. Add in the tea and continue to reduce the syrup for about 10 minutes. Remove from heat and strain into a heatproof container.

Immediately after removing the cake from the oven, poke holes all over the cake with a wooden skewer and brush with about a third of the simple syrup. Let cool in the pan for 10 minutes, then invert onto a wire rack or serving plate. Brush the tops and sides of the cake with the remaining syrup. Cool completely before glazing.

Make the Lemon Glaze: Sift the icing sugar into a small bowl. Whisk in the salt, butter, milk, and lemon juice. Whisk until smooth, adding more lemon juice 1 teaspoon at a time as needed to create a thick but pourable glaze. Use immediately, drizzling or spooning over the cooled cake as desired. Allow the glaze to set for about 10 minutes before serving. Store leftovers in an airtight container at room temperature for up to 5 days.

STRAWBERRY–ELDERFLOWER FRAISIER

MAKES ONE 6–INCH (15–CM) CAKE

I look forward to Ontario strawberry season every year because it signals the unofficial start of summer. It also gives me an excuse to make a *fraisier*, a traditional French strawberries-and-cream cake. To me, this cake is the best way to enjoy candy-sweet, in-season strawberries (after eating them straight off the plant). Use the absolute finest strawberries you can find—they should be beautifully red all the way through. A touch of elderflower liqueur adds a pleasantly floral note to this simple but sophisticated cake.

CHIFFON CAKE
75 g (⅔ cup minus 1 tbsp) cake flour
90 g (⅓ cup plus 2 tbsp) granulated sugar (preferably caster), divided
¾ tsp baking powder
¼ tsp kosher salt
60 g (¼ cup) water
40 g (2 tbsp plus 2 tsp) neutral vegetable oil, such as grapeseed or canola
½ tsp pure vanilla extract
2 large egg yolks, at room temperature
3 large egg whites, at room temperature
¼ tsp cream of tartar

ELDERFLOWER SIMPLE SYRUP
50 g (¼ cup) granulated sugar
60 g (¼ cup) water
15 g (1 tbsp) elderflower liqueur (such as St-Germain)

Make the Chiffon Cake: Preheat the oven to 350°F (175°C) with a rack in the lower third. Line an 8-inch (20-cm) round cake pan with at least 3-inch (7.5-cm) sides with parchment and lightly grease the parchment, but otherwise do not grease the pan.

Sift together the cake flour, 65 grams (⅓ cup) of sugar, baking powder, and salt in a large, wide bowl. Whisk to combine. Make a well in the center of the dry ingredients. Add the water, oil, vanilla, and egg yolks to the well, and whisk until smooth.

In the bowl of a stand mixer fitted with the whisk attachment (or using a handheld mixer), beat the egg whites and cream of tartar on medium-low speed until foamy. Increase the speed to medium, and whisk until soft peaks form. With the mixer still on medium, slowly add the remaining 25 grams (2 tbsp) of sugar. Increase the mixer speed to medium-high and beat until you have glossy, firm peaks.

Using a flexible spatula, carefully fold the egg whites into the egg yolk batter one third at a time. Mix just until the batter is homogeneous and no white streaks remain.

Scrape the batter into the prepared pan and smooth the surface with an offset spatula. Give the pan a couple raps on the counter to dislodge any big air bubbles.

Bake until the cake is puffed and golden and a skewer inserted in the center comes out clean, about 25 to 30 minutes. Cool completely in the pan on a wire rack. Once cooled, run a thin spatula around the edge of the cake to loosen, then carefully turn out of the pan. Wrap the cake in plastic wrap and chill before assembling, at least 30 minutes.

Make the Elderflower Simple Syrup: In a small saucepan, bring the sugar and water to a boil over medium-high heat. Reduce the heat to low and simmer for about 2 minutes. Remove from the heat and add the elderflower liqueur. Pour into a heatproof container and cool to room temperature.

(Continued)

ELDERFLOWER CREAM DIPLOMAT

½ tsp powdered gelatin

255 g (1 cup plus 1 tbsp) whole milk, divided

50 g (¼ cup) granulated sugar, divided

Pinch of salt

22 g (scant 3 tbsp) cornstarch or custard powder

2 large egg yolks

14 g (1 tbsp) unsalted butter, cold and cubed

25 g (2 tbsp) elderflower liqueur

120 g (½ cup) heavy cream, cold

TO FINISH

10–12 whole strawberries, halved lengthwise

150 g (1 cup) chopped strawberries, mixed with 40 g (2 tbsp) strawberry preserves or jam

Additional strawberries, for garnishing

Make the Elderflower Cream Diplomat: Place a strainer over a large heat-safe bowl. In a small bowl, sprinkle the gelatin evenly over 15 grams (1 tbsp) of cold milk and allow to bloom while you prepare the rest of the pastry cream.

Off heat, combine the remaining milk, 40 grams (3½ tbsp) of sugar, and a pinch of salt in a medium saucepan.

In a medium bowl, whisk together the remaining 10 grams (2 tsp) of sugar and the cornstarch. Pour in about 2 tablespoons of the milk mixture and whisk to form a smooth paste. Add the egg yolks and whisk until smooth.

Heat the milk over medium heat until steaming. Remove from the heat. Pour the milk in a slow, steady stream into the egg yolk mixture, whisking constantly. Scrape the custard mixture back into the saucepan and return to medium heat. Cook, whisking constantly, until the mixture thickens and large bubbles appear on the surface. Once the bubbles appear, turn the heat down to medium-low and continue whisking on the heat for 2 minutes.

Remove the custard from the heat and whisk in the bloomed gelatin. Once the gelatin has dissolved, whisk in the butter and elderflower liqueur. Strain the pastry cream into the prepared bowl. Press a piece of plastic wrap against the surface of the pastry cream and cool to room temperature.

Once the pastry cream has cooled, whip the heavy cream to medium peaks. Whisk the pastry cream to loosen, then use a flexible spatula to gently fold the whipped cream into the pastry cream in three additions.

Transfer the cream diplomat to a piping bag fitted with a plain round tip and refrigerate while you continue assembling the cake.

Assemble the Fraisier: Using a sharp serrated knife, cut the cake in half horizontally into two even layers. Use a 6 x 3-inch (15 x 7.5-cm) cake ring to stamp out a 6-inch (15-cm) round from each layer. Clean the cake ring, then line with acetate and place on a cake board or plate.

Place one layer of the cake in the bottom of the ring and brush generously with the simple syrup. Place the halved strawberries, cut side out and pointed end up, around the edge of the pan. Pipe the cream diplomat between the fruits and in a single layer across the top of the cake. Use an offset palette knife to smooth the cream. Fill the center with the chopped strawberries and jam mixture, then cover with another layer of cream, reserving about 2 tablespoons of the cream for the top of the cake. Place the second layer of cake on top and press down to level. Soak with the simple syrup, then spread the reserved cream across the top. Refrigerate until set, about 4 hours.

Just before serving, remove the cake ring and acetate. Decorate the top with additional strawberries as desired. The cake is best served within 24 hours of assembly.

VARIATIONS

Individual Parfaits: Cut the cake into 1-inch (2.5-cm) cubes and divide among six small glasses. Soak with the syrup, then layer with chopped strawberries and cream diplomat. Top with fresh strawberries and a dollop of whipped cream, if desired.

Lemon: To make a lemon chiffon cake, reduce the water to 30 grams (2 tbsp). Add 30 grams (2 tbsp) of freshly squeezed lemon juice and the zest of 1 lemon in with the wet ingredients.

Cocoa: To make a cocoa chiffon cake, replace the water with 60 grams (¼ cup) of room-temperature coffee. Reduce the flour to 65 grams (½ cup) and sift 15 grams (2 tbsp) of Dutch-processed cocoa powder in with the dry ingredients.

Strawberry-Basil: Before making the pastry cream, bring the milk and 6 whole basil sprigs to a simmer in a medium saucepan over medium-low heat. Simmer for about 15 minutes, stirring occasionally, then remove from heat and cover. Allow the basil to steep for about 45 minutes. Strain the milk, adding more to reach 240 grams (1 cup), if necessary, and return to the saucepan along with 40 grams (3½ tbsp) of sugar, and a pinch of salt. Proceed as directed, omitting the elderflower liqueur in the pastry cream and the simple syrup. Add fresh basil leaves to the top for garnishing.

BAKER'S NOTES

A cake ring and acetate are the best tools to create a beautiful, clean edge on this cake. Both are readily available at baking supply stores and online suppliers. In a pinch, you can use a similar-sized springform pan and plastic wrap or parchment, but the results will not be as neat.

CHERRY–TOPPED CHEESECAKE

MAKES ONE 8–INCH (20–CM)
CHEESECAKE

GRAHAM CRACKER CRUST
175 g (1¾ cups) graham cracker
crumbs

25 g (2 tbsp) light brown sugar

Pinch of kosher salt

56 g (4 tbsp) unsalted butter,
melted

CHEESECAKE FILLING
500 g (2 blocks) full-fat cream
cheese, at room temperature

150 g (¾ cup) granulated sugar

½ tsp kosher salt

15 g (1 tbsp) pure vanilla extract

30 g (2 tbsp) lemon juice, freshly
squeezed

240 g (1 cup) full-fat sour cream, at
room temperature

3 large eggs, at room temperature

CHERRY TOPPING
8 g (1 tbsp) cornstarch

15 g (1 tbsp) cold water

340 g (2 cups) frozen sweet cherries

50 g (¼ cup) granulated sugar

30 g (2 tbsp) lemon juice, freshly
squeezed

Pinch of salt

¼ tsp pure almond extract

Cheesecakes have the reputation for being finicky to make. I'm here to tell you that it's really not that hard if you follow two of my golden rules: Use room temperature ingredients, and bake it low and slow. This classic cheesecake can be paired with whatever you like, but a crown of glistening cherries is my personal topping of choice.

Make the Graham Cracker Crust: Preheat the oven to 350°F (175°C) with one rack in the middle and one below. Grease an 8-inch (20-cm) round cake pan with at least 3-inch (7.5-cm) sides and line the bottom with parchment paper.

Stir together the cracker crumbs, sugar, salt, and melted butter. The mixture should hold together if you squeeze it in your hand. If the mixture doesn't hold together, add more melted butter 1 teaspoon at a time until it does. If overly greasy, add more cracker crumbs, 1 teaspoon at a time, until you get the right texture.

Press the cookie crumbs into the bottom of the pan, using a measuring cup or shot glass to compact the crumbs firmly and evenly. Bake until just set, about 10 minutes. Allow to cool completely on a wire rack.

Make the Cheesecake Filling: Lower the oven temperature to 275°F (135°C). Combine the cream cheese, sugar, and salt in the bowl of a food processor. Pulse until combined. Scrape down the sides, add the vanilla and lemon juice, and pulse until smooth. Add the sour cream and pulse until smooth. Scrape down the sides. Add the eggs one at a time, pulsing after each just to combine. Scrape down the sides and fold the batter a few times to make sure it's well combined.

Pour the batter into the pan with the prepared crust. Tap the pan on the counter several times to dislodge any large air bubbles. Transfer the cheesecake to the middle rack in the oven. On the rack below, place a roasting pan or 9 x 13–inch (23 x 33–cm) baking pan filled with about 2 inches (5 cm) of hot water.

Bake for 80 to 90 minutes, or until the edges of the cheesecake are set and puffed but the very center still wobbles like set gelatin. Turn off the oven, crack open the oven door, and allow the cheesecake to cool for at least 1 hour.

Remove the cooled cheesecake from the oven. Run an offset spatula around the edges to loosen (but keep the cake in its pan) and cool to room temperature on a wire rack. Refrigerate at least 4 hours, preferably overnight, before serving. To release the cake from the pan, lay a piece of plastic on a flat plate at least 8 inches (20 cm) wide. Run an offset spatula around the cake, invert onto the plastic-lined plate, remove the parchment, and reinvert onto a serving plate.

Make the Cherry Topping: In a small bowl, mix together the cornstarch and water. Set aside. In a medium saucepan, combine the cherries, sugar, lemon juice, and salt. Cook over medium-low heat, stirring constantly, until the mixture comes to a simmer. Once the mixture reaches a simmer, add the cornstarch slurry. Continue cooking until the juices thicken and turn translucent, about 2 minutes. Transfer to a heatproof container and stir in the almond extract. Cool to room temperature, then refrigerate until ready to use. Right before serving, spoon cherries on top of cheesecake. Refrigerate leftover cheesecake in an airtight container for up to 3 days.

VARIATIONS

Sour Cream Topping: Mix 240 grams (1 cup) of sour cream and 15 grams (2 tbsp) of powdered sugar until smooth. Spread over the top of the chilled cheesecake after it has been transferred to a serving platter.

Pumpkin: Combine 285 grams (1¼ cups) of pumpkin puree, 200 grams (1 cup) of brown sugar, and 4 grams (2 tsp) of pumpkin pie spice in a medium saucepan. Cook over medium heat until sputtering; continue cooking until thick and shiny, about 5 minutes. Cool to room temperature, then mix the cheesecake batter as directed, omitting the granulated sugar and lemon juice and adding the pumpkin mixture after the sour cream. Top with whipped cream.

Fruit Swirl: Right before baking, drizzle about 60 grams (3 tbsp) of fruit jam, such as the Quick Berry Jam (page 48), over the top of the cheesecake batter. Use a toothpick or skewer to swirl it in

MOM'S SPONGE CAKE

MAKES ONE 10–INCH (25–CM) TUBE CAKE

188 g (1½ cups) cake flour

300 g (1½ cups) granulated sugar (preferably superfine), divided

110 g (½ cup) neutral vegetable oil, such as grapeseed or canola

½ tsp kosher salt

10 g (2 tsp) pure vanilla extract

10 large eggs, separated when cold but brought to room temperature before mixing the batter

¼ tsp cream of tartar

This cake is a treasure from my mom's recipe box. My mom didn't do a lot of baking when I was growing up (she was extremely busy raising five kids!), but she was a master at making this beautifully tender sponge cake. To this day it remains one of my favorite cakes—soft and fluffy as a cloud, and simply perfect any time of the day.

Preheat the oven to 350°F (175°C) with a rack in the lower third. Sift the cake flour into a small bowl and set aside.

In a large, wide mixing bowl, combine 150 grams (¾ cup) of the sugar, oil, salt, vanilla, and egg yolks and beat on medium with an electric mixer or by hand with a balloon whisk until creamy and the sugar is dissolved, 2 to 3 minutes with a mixer or longer if by hand. Set aside.

In the bowl of a stand mixer fitted with the whisk attachment, beat the egg whites and cream of tartar on medium-low until foamy. Increase the speed to medium. When the whites reach soft peak stage, slowly add the remaining 150 grams (¾ cup) of sugar, a spoonful at a time. Once all the sugar has been added, increase the speed to medium-high and whip until the mixture is glossy and holds medium-stiff peaks.

Sift the flour into the yolk mixture in three batches, using a flexible spatula to mostly fold each portion in before sifting in the next. Once all the flour has been added, continue folding until all the flour is incorporated and the mixture is thick and smooth. Be sure to scoop all the way down to the bottom of the bowl to make sure no pockets of flour remain.

Fold in the whipped egg whites in three portions, using a flexible spatula to mostly fold in each portion before adding the next. Once all the egg whites have been added, fold until the batter is smooth and uniform in color, taking care not to overmix.

Pour the batter into an ungreased aluminum 10-inch (25-cm) tube pan. (Don't use a non-stick pan, as this style of cake needs to cling to the sides to rise.) Bake for 50 to 60 minutes or until the cake is well browned and a skewer inserted near the center comes out clean. Do not open the oven door for at least 45 minutes or the delicate cake may fall.

Invert the pan to cool completely (if your pan doesn't have feet, you can insert a funnel or heavy bottle through the center). Once cool, slide an offset spatula around the edges to loosen, remove the insert, then slide the spatula around the bottom. Flip the cake onto a serving platter. Store leftovers in an airtight container at room temperature for up to 5 days.

VARIATIONS

Lemon: Add the zest of 2 lemons to the egg yolk mixture and replace 1 teaspoon of the vanilla with lemon oil. Serve with dollops of whipped cream and Meyer Lemon Curd (page 79).

Layer Cake: This batter can be split into two 8 x 3-inch (20 x 7.5-cm) cake pans (about 30 minutes bake time) or three 8 x 2-inch (20 x 5-cm) pans (about 25 minutes bake time). Line the bottoms of the pans with parchment but don't grease the sides, and cool the cakes completely in the pan before removing.

Fruity Whipped Cream Topping: A batch of fruity whipped cream is a lovely accompaniment for this light cake. Stir about 15 to 30 grams of finely ground freeze-dried fruit (from about ½ to 1 cup of freeze-dried fruit pieces) and 50 grams (¼ cup) of granulated sugar into 480 grams (2 cups) of heavy cream before whipping. For an extra-thick mixture that can hold up as a frosting, whip in a food processor (watch it very closely, as the food processor is much faster than a regular mixer).

BAKER'S NOTES

One of the most important keys to success with sponge cakes is properly whipped egg whites. I have the best success starting on a low speed and gradually raising it; this helps build a tighter, more stable structure and helps reduce the possibility of overbeating.

THE STAFF OF LIFE: YEASTED *and* SOURDOUGH BREADS

If I had to choose only one type of baked good to make for the rest of my life, it would be bread. I never tire of watching the most basic ingredients transform into a shiny-crusted, well-risen loaf. A slice of fresh Hearth Bread (page 96) or Honey Whole-Wheat Rolls (page 98) with a smear of butter is truly one of life's pleasures!

I firmly believe that anyone can learn to make bread. With a basic understanding of fermentation, a few versatile recipes, and practice, you can possess all the tools you need to craft loaves for any occasion. In this chapter, I'll walk you through my go-to formulas for everyday breads, filled buns, and decorative loaves. I've included recipes using yeast, but also several for sourdough (my favorite!), including our Nearly Naked Sourdough Focaccia (page 106) and Braided Sourdough Challah (page 121).

A NOTE ON YEAST
For the yeasted breads in this chapter, I call for instant (not quick-rise or rapid-rise) yeast. You can substitute the same amount of active dry yeast; rising times may be a touch longer.

For the sourdough breads in this chapter, you'll need an active 100-percent-hydration sourdough starter (equal parts flour and water). You can make your own starter, buy it online, or see if your local artisan bakery sells their starter.

A NOTE ON THE WINDOWPANE TEST
Some of these recipes will instruct you to mix or knead the dough until it passes the windowpane test. To perform the windowpane test, tear off a cherry-sized piece of dough and gently stretch it. If you can stretch the dough to form a thin, translucent membrane (a "windowpane") without it breaking, you're done kneading. If it tears before reaching that stage, keep kneading and check every 1 to 2 minutes until the dough passes the test.

HEARTH BREAD

MAKES ONE LARGE LOAF

When my kids and I visit our neighborhood bakery, I usually let them pick a treat. My son routinely walks past the cookies and pastries and chooses an Italian-style roll. I was determined to make something similar that would garner the same enthusiasm. This is it—a crusty-but-not-too-crusty loaf with a soft yet chewy crumb.

STARTER
125 g (1 cup) bread flour
125 g (1 cup) all-purpose flour
⅛ tsp instant yeast
164 g (⅔ cup plus 1 tsp) water, at room temperature

FINAL DOUGH
200 g (1⅓ cups) bread flour
62 g (½ cup) all-purpose flour
12 g (1 tbsp) sugar
9 g (2¼ tsp) kosher salt
1 tsp instant yeast
All the starter
24 g (1 tbsp plus 2 tsp) olive oil
153 g (½ cup plus 2 tbsp) water, at room temperature
Semolina or cornmeal, for dusting
Rice flour, for dusting (optional)

Make the Starter: In a medium bowl, mix the flours, yeast, and water to form a stiff dough. Let ferment at room temperature until doubled, 10 to 12 hours.

Mix the Final Dough: In a large bowl, whisk together the flours, sugar, salt, and yeast. Cut or tear the starter into eight pieces and add to the bowl, along with the olive oil and water. Stir until the ingredients form a ball.

Knead in the bowl with your hands (or with a stand mixer fitted with a dough hook) until the dough is smooth and supple, about 8 to 10 minutes by hand (about 5 minutes with a mixer). The dough should be soft but not sticky. Transfer the dough to an oiled container and cover with a tea towel or plastic wrap. Allow to rise at room temperature until doubled, approximately 60 to 90 minutes.

Shape, Proof, and Bake the Loaf: Turn the dough out onto a lightly floured surface and gently shape into a loose round. Cover with a large bowl or lightly oiled plastic and let rest for 10 minutes. Meanwhile, line a large baking sheet or (if baking directly on a baking steel or stone) pizza peel with parchment paper and lightly dust the parchment with semolina flour or cornmeal.

To shape the loaf, flip the dough over so the smooth side is down. Gently pat into a rough rectangle. With a short side facing you, fold the top third down two-thirds of the way. Press firmly to seal. Turn the dough 180 degrees and repeat. Fold the top of the dough down to the bottom and pinch to seal. Turn the dough so the seam side is down and gently roll the dough to about 12 inches (30 cm) in length. Transfer the loaf to the prepared baking sheet or peel, placing it seam side down. Cover with lightly oiled plastic wrap.

Allow the dough to proof at room temperature until it has increased by about 50 percent, about 45 to 60 minutes. If you poke the loaf gently with a floured finger, the indentation should fill back in very slowly. Meanwhile, preheat the oven to 500°F (260°C) with a baking stone on the center rack (if you have one) and a sheet tray or cast-iron pan on the rack below or the bottom of the oven.

When the loaf is ready to bake, have ready a measuring glass filled with hot water, just off the boil. Lightly dust the top of the loaf with rice flour, if desired. Using a sharp blade, slash the top down the center or score as desired.

Transfer the loaf to the oven (either on the baking sheet or, if using a pizza peel, directly onto the baking stone) and very carefully pour about a cup of the hot water into the preheated sheet tray or pan. Bake for 5 minutes, then turn the heat down to 450°F (230°C) and bake for another 15 to 20 minutes, rotating the loaf 180 degrees halfway through baking. When done, the loaf should be well browned and sound hollow when tapped on the bottom. Transfer to a wire rack to cool completely before slicing.

VARIATIONS

Semolina Sesame: Replace 75 grams (⅔ cup) of the bread flour in the final dough with semolina flour. After shaping the loaf, mist with water and sprinkle with untoasted white sesame seeds. Proof and bake as directed.

Individual Rolls: Instead of shaping one large loaf, divide the dough into eight equal pieces. Shape into round or oval rolls and bake as directed; rolls will bake a bit faster (about 15 to 20 minutes total) than one large loaf.

Garlic Bread: Combine 113 grams (½ cup) of softened unsalted butter, 15 grams (1 tbsp) of olive oil, 9 grams (1 tbsp) of finely minced fresh garlic, ½ teaspoon of kosher salt, ¼ teaspoon of black pepper, and ¼ cup of chopped fresh parsley and mix well. Slice the baked loaf in half horizontally and spread the butter evenly over each half. For crisp garlic bread, bake the cut sides up in a preheated 400°F (200°C) oven for about 10 to 15 minutes or until golden brown. For soft garlic bread, reassemble the loaf, buttered sides touching, and wrap in foil; bake in a preheated 400°F (200°C) oven for about 15 minutes or until butter is melted and bread is soft.

BAKER'S NOTES

If using a sheet tray for steaming, choose a clean but old one. The pan can warp over time so I reserve my most tired-looking pan for this task. Alternatively, if you have a large roasting pan long enough to cover the loaf, you can create steam by inverting the pan over the loaf like a lid for the first 12 minutes of baking, then removing it for the remainder of the baking time.

Leftover bread can be stored in a paper bag at room temperature for up to 2 days.

HONEY WHOLE-WHEAT ROLLS

MAKES 16 ROLLS

250 g (2 cups) bread flour
125 g (1 cup) whole-wheat flour
42 g (⅓ cup) all-purpose flour
8 g (2 tsp) kosher salt
6 g (2 tsp) instant yeast
282 g (1 cup plus 3 tbsp) buttermilk, at room temperature
1 large egg, at room temperature
40 g (2 tbsp) honey
42 g (3 tbsp) unsalted butter, at room temperature
1 large egg, whisked with 1 tsp milk or water and a pinch of salt, for egg wash
Sesame and/or poppy seeds, for garnishing (optional)
Melted unsalted butter, for brushing (optional)

This is my formula for soft and tender pull-apart dinner rolls, perfect alongside a bowl of soup or as part of a breadbasket. The combination of whole-wheat flour, buttermilk, and honey creates a remarkably flavorful bun that keeps well for several days. These rolls come together in an afternoon, so you can start mixing the dough after lunch and have these on the table for dinner.

Mix the Dough: In the bowl of a stand mixer fitted with the dough hook, stir together the flours, salt, and yeast. Whisk together the buttermilk, egg, and honey, and pour over the dry ingredients. Mix on low until the ingredients come together in a ball, scraping down the sides as needed to incorporate all the flour.

Raise the speed to medium-low and mix until the dough is soft, supple, and clears the bottom of the bowl, about 3 to 5 minutes. Turn the mixer down to low and add the butter about 1 tablespoon at a time, incorporating each batch completely before adding the next. Once all the butter has been added, increase the speed to medium-low and mix until the dough is smooth, supple, and holds together in a ball, about 8 to 10 minutes. It should be tacky but not overly sticky and pass the windowpane test. Shape the dough into a smooth ball and transfer to a lightly oiled container. Cover the container with a lint-free tea towel or plastic wrap. Let the dough rise at room temperature until doubled in size, about 60 minutes.

Shape, Proof, and Bake the Rolls: Once doubled, carefully turn the dough out onto a clean work surface. Divide into sixteen equal pieces, about 52 grams each. Form into loose rounds and cover with lightly oiled plastic for 5 minutes to rest. Meanwhile, line a baking sheet with parchment paper.

Working one at a time, reshape each piece into a tight, smooth ball by flattening each piece into a circle, then bringing the edges toward the center and pinching to seal. Place the ball seam side down on a clean, non-floured surface and cup your hand over it. Press firmly down while rotating your hand in a circular motion to tighten the surface of the dough. Transfer the shaped roll to the prepared sheet, seam side down. Repeat with remaining dough. Place the shaped rolls closely together; the rolls will grow into each other during proofing, creating pull-apart rolls with soft sides.

Cover with lightly oiled plastic and allow the buns to proof until they're roughly doubled in size, about 45 to 60 minutes. If you poke a roll gently with a floured finger, the indentation should fill back in very slowly. Towards the end of proofing, preheat the oven to 400°F (200°C) with a rack in the middle.

Right before baking, brush the rolls with the egg wash and sprinkle with sesame or poppy seeds, if desired. Bake for about 15 to 20 minutes, or until golden brown. The center of a roll should register at least 195°F (91°C) on an instant-read thermometer.

Remove from the oven and transfer to a wire rack. Brush with melted butter, if desired. Serve the rolls warm or at room temperature. Store leftovers in a sealed plastic bag to retain softness for up to 3 days.

VARIATIONS

Burger Buns: After the first rise, divide the dough into ten equal pieces, about 83 grams each. Rest for 5 minutes, then form into rounds. Place the buns on a parchment-lined baking sheet about 3 inches (7.5 cm) apart, then gently press down on the tops to create the desired bun shape. Proof and bake as directed.

Hot Dog Buns: After the first rise, divide the dough into ten equal pieces, about 83 grams each. Rest for 5 minutes, then form into logs about 5 inches (13 cm) long, and slightly flatten the tops. Place the logs close together (for soft-sided buns) on a baking sheet. Proof and bake as directed.

Sandwich Loaf: After the first rise, form the dough into a loose round and rest for 5 minutes. Shape into a 9-inch (23-cm) log and place into a lightly greased 9 x 5-inch (23 x 12-cm) loaf pan or 9 x 4-inch (23 x 10-cm) Pullman pan. Proof as directed. Bake at 400°F (200°C) for 20 minutes, then reduce the heat to 350°F (175°C) and bake for another 10 to 15 minutes, or until the loaf sounds hollow when tapped and a digital thermometer registers at least 195°F (91°C) in the center of the loaf. Remove from the pan and cool on a wire rack.

BAKER'S NOTES

You can also bake these rolls in two lightly greased 8-inch (20-cm) or 9-inch (23-cm) round cake pans or a 9 x 13-inch (23 x 33-cm) pan. If using round cake pans, arrange eight buns per pan, giving space for each (they'll grow into each other during proofing). For a 9 x 13-inch (23 x 33-cm) pan, divide the dough into fifteen pieces and arrange in three rows of five buns each. If baking in cake pans rather than on a baking sheet, remove the buns from the pans to cool on a wire rack to keep the bottoms from getting soggy.

ZA'ATAR BRIOCHE WREATH

MAKES ONE 8–INCH
(20–CM) BRAID

BRIOCHE DOUGH
250 g (2 cups) bread flour

125 g (1 cup) all-purpose flour

38 g (3 tbsp) granulated sugar

7 g (1¾ tsp) kosher salt

5 g (1½ tsp) instant yeast

3 large eggs, cold

1 large egg yolk, cold (reserve white for egg wash)

60 g (¼ cup) whole milk, cold

150 g (10½ tbsp) unsalted butter, cool but pliable

ZA'ATAR FILLING
3 g (1 tbsp) dried thyme

5 g (1 tbsp) ground coriander

8 g (1 tbsp) ground cumin

8 g (1 tbsp) ground sumac

3 g (1 tsp) toasted sesame seeds

½ tsp kosher salt

60 g (4 tbsp) olive oil

FOR FINISHING
1 large egg white, whisked with 1 tsp water and a pinch of salt, for egg wash

Flaky salt

There's no bread quite like brioche, with its golden hue and tender, melt-in-the-mouth crumb. It's also an incredibly versatile dough that can be baked as plain loaves or shaped and stuffed any way you like it. Here, I've taken a savory turn and spread the dough with za'atar, an aromatic Middle Eastern spice blend.

Mix the Brioche Dough: Combine the flours, sugar, salt, yeast, eggs, yolk, and milk in the bowl of a stand mixer fitted with the dough hook. Mix on low for 3 to 4 minutes to combine, scraping down the sides occasionally to ensure all the flour is incorporated. Once the dough has come together, continue mixing on low for 4 to 5 minutes—it will be smooth and stiff at this point.

With the mixer running on low, add the butter about 2 tablespoons at a time, waiting for each addition to incorporate before adding the next. Scrape down the sides of the bowl as necessary. Be patient; it can take up to 15 minutes to incorporate all the butter.

Once all the butter has been incorporated, turn the mixer up to medium and continue mixing for about 15 to 20 minutes, or until the dough clears the bottom and sides of the bowl in a single mass and the gluten is very well developed. Stop the mixer and scrape down the bowl and dough hook a few times during this process. At the end of mixing, the dough should be very soft, shiny, and supple. You should be able to pick it up all in one piece.

Transfer the dough to a lightly oiled container. Cover and let rise at room temperature for 1 hour. Stretch and fold each side into the center, then cover and refrigerate for at least 8 hours, or up to 18 hours, before using.

Shape and Bake the Wreath: Before shaping the dough, mix together the thyme, coriander, cumin, sumac, sesame seeds, salt, and olive oil together. Turn the chilled dough out onto a lightly floured surface and roll into a large rectangle about 12 x 16 inches (30 x 41 cm), turning and flipping the dough occasionally to maintain an even thickness. Brush any extra flour off the dough, then use an offset spatula to spread the filling evenly over the entire surface. Starting from a long edge, roll the dough tightly like a jelly roll. Pinch the seam well to seal, then turn the dough seam side down and gently roll back and forth a few times to even out the log. If the dough feels soft at this point, chill for about 10 minutes.

Move the log to a piece of parchment and have an 8-inch (20-cm) round cake pan with 3-inch (7.5-cm)-high sides ready. Using a sharp knife or bench scraper, cut the dough in half lengthwise. Position the two strips side-by-side, cut sides up. Pinch the top ends together, then twist the strands together by repeatedly lifting one over the other to make a long two-stranded braid, always keeping the cut sides exposed. Pinch the bottom ends to seal, then coil the twist up into a spiral, again keeping the cut sides exposed. Transfer, still on the parchment, to the cake pan. Cover with lightly oiled plastic and allow to proof at room temperature until quite puffy (but not necessarily doubled), about 90 minutes.

About 30 minutes before baking, preheat the oven to 400°F (200°C) with a rack in the lower third. Right before baking, brush with the egg wash and sprinkle with flaky salt. Bake for 5 minutes, then lower the temperature to 350°F (175°C) and continue baking for about 40 to 55 minutes longer, or until the top is golden brown and an instant-read thermometer registers at least 195°F (91°C) in the center. Check the loaf after about 20 minutes; if it appears to be browning too quickly, tent with foil.

Allow the brioche to cool in the pan for 10 minutes, then remove and transfer to a wire rack to cool completely. Brioche is best served the day it's baked, but leftovers can be stored in a plastic bag at room temperature for up to 3 days.

BAKER'S NOTES

Because this dough is highly enriched and gets extremely sticky during mixing, I don't recommend trying to knead by hand.

Brioche tends to brown quickly during baking, so I recommend checking the internal temperature to determine doneness.

VARIATIONS

Sweet Fillings: Replace the za'atar seasoning with ½ to ⅔ cup of fruit jam or Nutella®.

Brioche Nanterre: For a plain loaf, divide the chilled dough into eight equal pieces and place in two staggered rows of four in a lightly greased 9 x 4-inch (23 x 10-cm) Pullman pan. Cover and proof until the dough has nearly reached the top of the pan (this may take 3 or more hours, depending on the temperature of your kitchen). Right before baking, brush with the egg wash and sprinkle with pearl sugar, if desired. Bake at 400°F (200°C) for 20 minutes, then lower the temperature to 350°F (175°C) and bake for another 20 to 25 minutes or until deeply golden and the internal temperature reaches 195°F (91°C) (tent with foil partway through if needed). Remove loaf from pan and cool on a wire rack.

Brioche Tarts: Divide the chilled dough into ten equal pieces and press down into 4-inch (10-cm) tart molds, or roll into 4-inch (10-cm) circles and place on a parchment-lined baking sheet. Cover and proof until the dough is puffed and, when poked, springs back very slowly (about 1½ to 2 hours). Firmly press down the centers, leaving a raised border around the edge. Fill the centers with Vanilla-Almond Pastry Cream (page 162) or Frangipane (page 166) and top with sliced peaches, plums, apples, or a dollop of jam. Brush the exposed dough with the egg wash and sprinkle with coarse or pearl sugar. Bake at 375°F (190°C) for about 20 minutes, or until the brioche is golden brown.

Brioche Doughnuts: Divide the chilled dough into ten to twelve equal pieces and form into smooth, tight balls. Place each round on an individual square of parchment on a baking sheet. Cover and proof until doubled, about 2 hours. When dough is nearly proofed, heat 3 to 4 inches (7.5 to 10 cm) of neutral vegetable oil to 350°F (175°C) in a heavy bottomed saucepan or Dutch oven. Place a cooling rack on a baking sheet lined with paper towels. Carefully transfer two or three doughnuts, parchment side up, into the oil. (The parchment will release on its own—remove with tongs and discard).

Fry the doughnuts for about 2½ to 3 minutes per side, or until puffed and golden. Remove from the oil and drain on the prepared rack. Repeat with the remaining dough. Cool to room temperature, then roll in granulated sugar, or your choice of flavored sugar sprinkle (page 32). If desired, use a chopstick to poke a hole in the sides and fill with pastry cream, jam, or fruit curd.

COCONUT COCKTAIL BUNS

MAKES 12 BUNS

TANGZHONG
25 g (3 tbsp) bread flour

125 g (½ cup) milk

DOUGH
225 g (1¾ cups plus 1 tbsp) bread flour

125 g (1 cup) all-purpose flour

46 g (3½ tbsp) sugar

7 g (1¾ tsp) kosher salt

21 g (3 tbsp) milk powder

6 g (2 tsp) instant yeast

63 g (¼ cup) heavy cream, at room temperature

63 g (¼ cup) milk, at room temperature

1 large egg, at room temperature

All the tangzhong

56 g (4 tbsp) unsalted butter, at room temperature

FILLING
168 g (12 tbsp) unsalted butter, at room temperature

74 g (⅓ cup plus 2 tsp) granulated sugar

¼ tsp kosher salt

47 g (⅓ cup plus 2 tsp) cake flour

56 g (8 tbsp) milk powder

90 g (1 cup) unsweetened desiccated coconut

TOPPING AND FINISHING
63 g (4½ tbsp) unsalted butter, at room temperature

38 g (3 tbsp) granulated sugar

60 g (scant ½ cup) cake flour

1 large egg, whisked with 1 tsp milk or water and a pinch of salt, for egg wash, divided

Sesame seeds, for garnishing

Simple syrup or warmed honey (optional)

My dad worked in Chinatown for decades, and when my brothers and I were young he'd occasionally bring home a bright pink box filled with Asian bakery treats. These coconut buns (or *gai mei bao*) were always a family favorite. The best part of gai mei bao is the buttery coconut filling, so I've packed a generous amount into this homemade version. The bread dough uses the "tangzhong" technique, which involves cooking a portion of the flour with liquid in order to give the bread a longer-lasting soft texture.

Make the Tangzhong: In a small saucepan, whisk the flour and milk together until smooth. Cook over medium-low heat, whisking constantly, until the mixture thickens enough for the whisk to leave lines on the bottom of the pan, about 5 minutes.

Transfer the tangzhong to a clean container and press plastic wrap directly on the surface to prevent a skin from forming. Let cool to room temperature before using.

Mix the Dough: In the bowl of a stand mixer fitted with the dough hook, combine the flours, sugar, salt, milk powder, yeast, cream, milk, egg, and tangzhong. Mix on medium-low until the dough is smooth, about 3 to 5 minutes.

Turn the mixer to low and add the butter about 1 tablespoon at a time, incorporating each batch before adding the next. Turn the speed up to medium and continue kneading until the dough is smooth and supple and passes the windowpane test, about 10 minutes.

Shape the dough into a smooth ball and transfer to a clean, lightly oiled container. Cover and let rise at warm room temperature, 78 to 80°F (26 to 27°C) until doubled, about 60 to 90 minutes.

While the dough is proofing, make the filling and topping.

Make the Filling and Topping: To make the filling, cream together the butter, sugar, and salt until well combined, about 2 to 3 minutes. Add the cake flour, milk powder, and coconut and mix to combine. Divide the mixture into 12 equal portions, about 36 grams each. Roll each portion into a short log about 3½ inches (9 cm) long. Cover until ready to use.

To make the topping, cream together the butter and sugar until smooth. Add the cake flour and mix well. Transfer the mixture to a re-sealable bag and snip off a corner for piping. (The mixture is rather thick and is easier to pipe from a re-sealable bag as opposed to a piping bag.)

(Continued)

COCONUT COCKTAIL BUNS (CONTINUED)

Fill, Shape, and Bake the Buns: Transfer the proofed dough to a clean floured surface. Gently deflate and divide the dough into twelve equal portions. Shape into smooth balls. Cover with lightly oiled plastic wrap and let rest for 10 minutes. Meanwhile, line a large baking sheet with parchment paper.

To shape a bun, turn the roll or press out a portion of the dough into an oval shape, about 3 x 5 inches (8 x 13 cm). Place a portion of filling in the middle of the oval lengthwise. Fold the dough in half and pinch the edges well to seal in the filling—make sure to really pinch tight so the filling doesn't leak out during baking! Turn the bun seam side down. Pinch the ends and gently roll back and forth a few times to seal well. Transfer to the prepared baking sheet, seam side down. Repeat with the remaining dough and filling.

Once all the buns are shaped, brush with the egg wash and cover with lightly oiled plastic wrap. Let proof at warm room temperature, 78 to 80°F (26 to 27°C) until noticeably puffy, about 45 to 60 minutes. Meanwhile, preheat the oven to 400°F (200°C) with a rack in the middle.

Right before baking, lightly brush the buns with a second coat of the egg wash. Pipe two stripes of topping on each bun, about 1 inch (2.5 cm) from each end. Sprinkle with sesame seeds.

Bake for about 18 to 20 minutes, or until golden brown. Remove from the oven and transfer to a wire rack. Brush the tops with simple syrup or warmed honey, if desired. Cool for about 10 minutes before serving. Buns are best slightly warm from the oven. Store leftover buns in a sealed plastic bag at room temperature for 2 to 3 days. Microwave them briefly to restore their soft texture.

VARIATIONS

Sandwich Loaf: This dough can be baked as a single loaf in a 9 x 5-inch (23 x 13-cm) loaf pan or a 9 x 4-inch (23 x 10-cm) Pullman pan. Omit the coconut filling and topping. Follow the directions for shaping in Soft Sourdough Sandwich Bread (page 114). Bake at 350°F (175°C) for about 30 to 40 minutes.

Curry Beef Buns: Substitute the coconut filling with Curry Beef Filling (page 136). Instead of flattening each dough portion into an oval, flatten into a round with the edges thinner than the middle. Place a generous spoonful of filling in the center. Pull the edges of the dough over the filling and pinch together well to seal in the filling. Place the buns seam side down. Proof and bake as directed, omitting the piped topping but garnishing with sesame seeds.

Cinnamon Rolls: This dough can be used to make a yeasted version of the sourdough cinnamon rolls or any of its variations. Follow the filling and shaping directions in Sourdough Cinnamon Rolls (page 118) and the proofing and baking times above.

BAKER'S NOTES

Desiccated coconut provides the best texture for the filling—it is finer than regular shredded coconut. If you can't find desiccated coconut, pulse an equal weight of shredded coconut in a food processor until fine.

NEARLY NAKED SOURDOUGH FOCACCIA

MAKES ONE
9 X 9–INCH
(23 X 23–CM) PAN

113 g (½ cup) active, ripe sourdough starter (100% hydration)

183 g (¾ cup) room temperature water

250 g (2 cups) bread flour

12 g (2 tbsp) rye flour

5 g (1¼ tsp) kosher salt

10 g (2 tsp) good quality olive oil, plus more for coating the pan and drizzling

Flaky sea salt, for sprinkling

About 1 tbsp fresh or 1 tsp dried chopped herbs, such as thyme or rosemary, for sprinkling (optional)

Nothing hits the spot quite like a fresh piece of focaccia fresh out of the oven. With a salted top, chewy interior, and crisp bottom, it's the perfect accompaniment to a bowl of soup or stew. Focaccia is also one of the simplest breads to make as you don't have to do much in terms of shaping or kneading. While you can top focaccia with anything you want, I like to keep it simple with flaky salt and herbs to let the flavor of the bread and olive oil really shine.

In a medium bowl, mix together the sourdough starter and water until the starter is dissolved. Add the flours and salt and mix to form a rough dough. Using a damp hand, knead in the bowl until the dough smooths out and holds together—about 3 to 5 minutes. Add the olive oil and pinch in to combine, then knead 2 to 3 minutes longer, or until all the ingredients are well incorporated.

Transfer the dough to an oiled container and cover with a lint-free tea towel or plastic wrap.

Let the dough rise at warm room temperature, 78 to 80°F (26 to 27°C) until doubled in size, about 2 to 3 hours.

Once the dough has doubled, coat the bottom of a 9 x 9–inch (23 x 23–cm) cake pan (preferably anodized aluminum, see Baker's Notes) with 2 to 3 tablespoons of olive oil. Make sure the oil covers the entire bottom of the pan—this will create a lovely crunchy bottom and keep the bread from sticking.

Using a damp hand, gently release the dough from the proofing container by carefully folding each of the sides in, then turn it into the center of the oiled pan, folded side down. Cover and let rest for about 45 to 60 minutes, or until the dough has relaxed out to mostly fill the pan and has roughly doubled in size again.

Using oiled fingers, gently press from the center of the dough to fill out the corners of the pan. It's okay if the corners aren't perfect.

Cover the dough and let rise at warm room temperature, 78 to 80°F (26 to 27°C) until very puffy and airy, about 2 to 3 hours. If using a 2-inch (5-cm)-high pan, the dough should come about halfway up the sides of the pan.

About 45 minutes before baking, preheat the oven to 500°F (260°C) with a rack and baking stone or steel, if you have one, in the center of the oven. Right after preheating the oven, drizzle the dough with olive oil and dimple it in with your fingertips, gently pressing down to the bottom of the pan. Sprinkle with flaky salt and herbs, if using. Let the focaccia rest, uncovered, while the oven finishes preheating.

Bake for 5 minutes, then lower the temperature to 450°F (230°C) and continue baking until golden brown, about 20 to 25 minutes longer.

Immediately turn the focaccia out of the pan onto a wire rack to cool. Focaccia is best served within 2 to 3 hours of baking, but leftovers can be wrapped in foil and re-warmed in an oven or toaster at a low temperature a day or two later.

VARIATIONS

Herb Oil: In a small saucepan, heat 220 grams (1 cup) of olive oil until just warm. Remove from the heat and add ½ cup of mixed, chopped fresh herbs (or a large handful of dried herbs), 3 cloves of chopped garlic, 6 grams (1½ tsp) of kosher salt, and a few grinds of fresh pepper. For best flavor, allow to steep for a day before using. Use this oil to drizzle on the bottom of the pan and on top of the focaccia; leftovers can be stored in the fridge for up to 6 months.

Sesame-Scallion: Replace the olive oil in the dough with toasted sesame oil. After dimpling the dough, sprinkle with 18 grams (2 tbsp) of sesame seeds, a handful of finely chopped scallions, and flaky salt. Sprinkle with additional chopped scallions after baking and serve with a dipping sauce made of equal parts soy sauce and black vinegar, plus a pinch of sugar and freshly grated ginger to taste.

Grape: After dimpling the dough, press in about 150 grams (1 cup) of halved black seedless or concord grapes and top with a sprinkling of coarse sugar, flaky sea salt, and chopped fresh rosemary.

Olive: After dimpling the dough, press in about 90 grams (½ cup) of pitted, coarsely chopped olives (whatever kind you prefer) and top with a sprinkling of flaky sea salt, freshly ground pepper, and chopped fresh thyme.

BAKER'S NOTES

This recipe was inspired by Nancy Silverton, though I have adjusted the method and adapted it for sourdough.

You can also bake this dough in an 8 x 8-inch (20 x 20-cm) cake pan for an extra-thick focaccia, or a 9-inch (23-cm) round cake pan. I recommend using anodized aluminum pans rather than glass or ceramic as they are less prone to sticking.

EVERYDAY SOURDOUGH LOAF

MAKES ONE LARGE LOAF

200 g (1⅔ cups) bread flour
100 g (¾ cup plus 1½ tsp) all-purpose flour
80 g (⅔ cup) whole-wheat flour
20 g (scant ¼ cup) rye flour
328 g (1¼ cups plus 2 tsp) room-temperature water, divided
80 g (⅓ cup) active, ripe sourdough starter (100% hydration)
9 g (2¼ tsp) kosher salt
Rice flour, for dusting

This is my signature sourdough bread. I bake it practically every week, and it is the loaf I gift to friends or bring along to potlucks. This bread bakes up with a cracker-thin, crisp crust but has a tender and flavorful crumb, thanks to a moderate amount of whole-grain flour. Whether simply smeared with butter or used as a base for fancier toppings, I never tire of this bread.

Mix the Dough: In a medium bowl, mix together the flours and 300 grams (1¼ cups) of the water. There's no need to knead—at this point you're just trying to hydrate all the flour, which will help kickstart gluten formation and reduce kneading time later. (This step is called the "autolyse.") Cover the bowl and let the dough sit at room temperature for at least 30 minutes or up to 3 hours.

Spread the ripe sourdough starter, along with half of the reserved water, on top of the dough. Use your fingers to pinch the starter into the dough. Fold the dough over itself and continue pinching in the starter for 1 to 2 minutes to incorporate everything evenly. The dough may break apart at first but should come back together as you continue pinching and folding. Cover the bowl again and let the dough rest for 20 minutes.

Sprinkle the salt on top, along with the remainder of the reserved water, if your flour can handle it. Each brand and variety of flour absorbs water differently, so you may not need to add all the reserved water. Only add enough water to get a soft but workable dough—it should not be soupy or overly sticky. Repeat the pinching and folding process for another 1 to 2 minutes, or until the salt is evenly dispersed. Once the salt is incorporated, start stretching the dough and folding it over itself, rotating the bowl a quarter turn after each fold. This is a gentle (and clean) way of developing the dough's strength. Stretch and fold the dough for about 3 to 5 minutes, or until the surface of the dough has smoothed out and holds together in a single mass. It should be fairly soft and tacky, but not overly sticky (if it is, keep folding for 1 to 2 minutes longer).

(Continued)

Use damp hands to lift up the side of the dough furthest away from you.	*Pull dough up and over toward the side nearest you.*	*Press down as if you were closing a book.*	*Repeat on all four sides.*

VARIATIONS

Whole-Grain Swap: The moderate amount of whole-wheat flour in this formula makes it a good testing ground for various whole grains. Replace the whole-wheat flour with another whole-grain flour such as spelt, emmer, einkorn, or kamut.

Seeded: Reduce the total water to 300 grams (1¼ cups) and autolyse the flour with 270 grams (1 cup plus 2 tbsp) of water. While the flour is autolysing, toast 60 grams (⅓ cup) of seeds (sesame, flax, poppy, millet, or a mix) in a dry skillet until fragrant. Transfer to a small bowl and cover with 60 grams (¼ cup) of hot water. Mix the soaked seeds into the dough along with the salt. After shaping, mist the top of the loaf with water and sprinkle on more seeds before transferring to the prepared proofing container.

Fruit and Nut: Mix in 60 grams (½ cup) of toasted, chopped nuts and 40 grams (¼ cup) of dried fruit (chopped, if large) along with the salt. The added sugars from the fruit can cause this loaf variation to brown more quickly; reduce the heat to 425°F (220°C) for the final 10 to 15 minutes of baking, if needed.

BAKER'S NOTES

Many home bakers like using a Dutch oven to bake crusty artisan-style loaves because the humid, sealed environment traps steam, which encourages maximal rise. Their excellent heat retention also helps the crust color quickly and richly. If you don't have a Dutch oven, you can use a baking steel or baking stone and a large roasting pan as a cover. Preheat both the steel or stone and the roasting pan along with the oven and bake as directed.

Transfer the dough to a lightly oiled container (I prefer a clear tub with straight sides so you can easily track the dough's rise). Cover with a tea towel and place in a warm spot. In addition to the strength of your starter, the temperature of your dough will dictate how quickly your dough will ferment. For this recipe, I try to keep my dough temperature around 78 to 80°F (26 to 27°C). I like to measure my dough temperature using a digital probe thermometer right at the end of mixing and after each fold.

Bulk ferment for 3 to 4 hours with stretch and folds every 30 minutes for the first 1 to 2 hours. Stretches and folds help to develop strength and structure and regulate the temperature of the dough. To stretch and fold, use damp hands to lift the side of the dough furthest away from you and pull it up and over the side facing you, as if you were closing a book. Turn the container 180 degrees and repeat. Repeat on the final three sides. (See step-by-step photos on page 108.)

Observe how the dough changes with each set of folds. After the third set of folds, if the dough feels noticeably less slack and is holding its shape, skip the last set of folds and let the dough sit, covered, for the rest of bulk fermentation. Conversely, if the dough feels weak or loose after three sets of folds, continue stretching and folding the dough every 30 minutes until you feel resistance when you fold. Bulk fermentation is done when the dough has increased by 30 to 50 percent, you can see fermentation bubbles along the bottom and sides of the container, and the edges are domed where the dough meets the container.

Shape, Proof, and Bake the Loaf: Lightly mist a clean worktop with oil. Gently turn the dough out and shape into a loose round. Let the dough rest, uncovered, for 20 minutes.

Prepare your banneton (or other proofing vessel, such as a kitchen bowl or colander) by lining it with a lint-free linen or cotton tea towel and lightly dusting the towel with rice flour. Lightly flour your work surface and the rested round. Use a bench scraper to flip your pre-shaped round over. Lightly dust your hands with flour and shape as desired, either into a *boule* (round) or *bâtard* (oval).

To Shape an Oval Loaf (Bâtard): Flip the pre-shaped round over so the smooth side is down. Stretch and pull the side closest to you about three-quarters of the way up and press to seal (Photos 1 & 2). Stretch and pull the left side of the dough over to the right and press to seal (Photo 3). Repeat with the right side (Photos 4 & 5). Stretch the top of the dough up and pull it to the bottom. Press to seal (Photos 6 & 7). You should have a squarish package of dough. Starting at the top of the square, pull small sections of dough from either side and criss-cross them over each other—this is called "stitching" the dough (Photos 8 & 9). Continue stitching all the way down the square, until the dough resembles a cocoon (Photo 10). Take the bottom of the dough and stretch it up and over the top, folding the cocoon in half (Photo 11). Use both hands to drag the dough toward you to tighten the shape and seal the seam (Photo 12). Lightly flour the top of the dough, then transfer seam side up to the prepared proofing vessel.

(Continued)

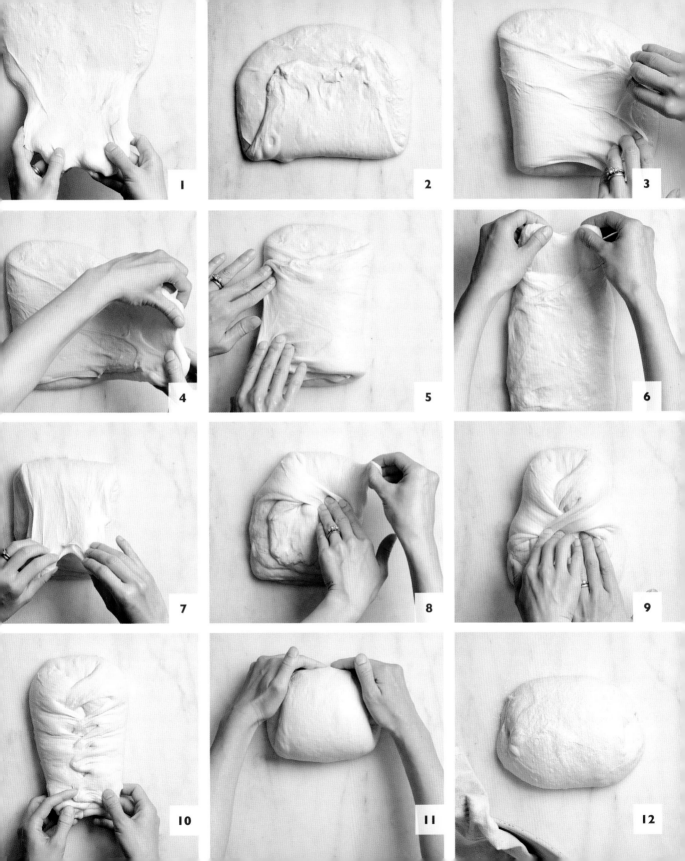

To Shape a Round Loaf (Boule): Flip the pre-shaped round over so the smooth side is down. Stretch and pull sections of the dough from the edge to the center, pressing to seal (Photos 1 & 2). Continue doing this around the entire perimeter of the dough (Photos 3, 4, & 5). Flip the dough over so the smooth side is up. Use both hands to drag the dough toward you to tighten the shape and seal the seam (Photos 6 & 7). Repeat several times, rotating the dough a little after each drag, until the top of the dough is smooth and you have a uniform shape. Lightly flour the top of the dough, then transfer seam side up to the prepared proofing vessel (Photo 8).

After shaping the dough, slip the proofing vessel with the dough into a large plastic bag or cover with lightly oiled plastic wrap. Let sit at room temperature for 20 minutes, then refrigerate overnight (at least 8 or up to 18 hours).

One hour before baking, preheat the oven to 500°F (260°C). For the best crust, bake this loaf in a Dutch oven (which you should preheat with the oven), or use your preferred method of steaming (see Baker's Notes). While the oven is preheating, remove the plastic covering from the loaf, but keep it refrigerated. This dries out the surface a little, making scoring easier.

When the oven is ready, carefully remove the preheated Dutch oven and take off the lid. Invert your loaf onto a piece of parchment on a pizza peel. Dust the top with rice flour, if desired. Using a sharp razor blade, lame, or scissors, score as desired. Carefully transfer the scored loaf to the Dutch oven and replace the lid. Bake at 500°F (260°C) for 20 minutes. Remove the lid, turn down the heat to 450°F (230°C), and bake for another 20 to 25 minutes or until your desired doneness, rotating a couple times for even baking. When finished, the crust should be richly browned and the loaf should sound hollow when tapped on the bottom.

Transfer to a wire rack and cool for at least 1 hour before cutting. Store leftovers in a paper bag at room temperature for up to 3 days.

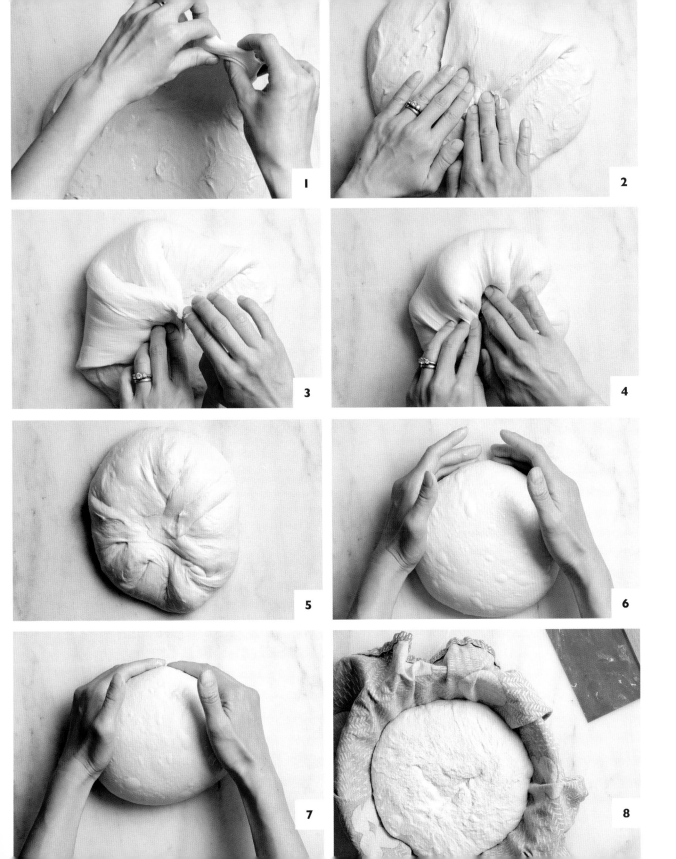

SOFT SOURDOUGH SANDWICH BREAD

MAKES ONE
9 X 4–INCH
(23 X 10–CM) LOAF

LEVAIN

18 g (1 heaping tbsp) ripe sourdough starter (100% hydration)

31 g (2 tbsp) whole milk

57 g (½ cup minus 2 tsp) bread flour

FINAL DOUGH

142 g (1 cup plus 2 tbsp) bread flour

142 g (1 cup plus 2 tbsp) all-purpose flour

35 g (2½ tbsp) granulated sugar

1 large egg

135 g (½ cup plus 1 tbsp) whole milk

21 g (3 tbsp) milk powder (optional)

All the levain

7 g (1¾ tsp) kosher salt

35 g (2½ tbsp) butter, softened

Milk, for brushing

Melted butter, for brushing (optional)

When I first started baking with sourdough, my son was just starting to eat solids but was still relatively toothless. I wanted to make a loaf that he could enjoy, and thus began my fascination with soft, enriched sourdough breads. Whereas lean, crusty loaves generally benefit from a light touch and minimal handling, enriched breads require more intense kneading and longer rising times as the added sugar and fat slows down fermentation. Patience is rewarded, though—this bread has a beautifully soft texture that makes picture-perfect sandwiches and delicious French toast. Note that this loaf requires a long levain build and two long proofs; I usually build the levain the night before I plan to mix the dough.

Make the Levain: In a medium bowl, mix the starter, milk, and flour together to form a stiff dough. Cover the bowl and ferment the levain at room temperature until more than doubled in volume, puffy, and domed, about 8 to 12 hours.

Mix the Final Dough: In the bowl of a stand mixer fitted with the dough hook, mix together the flours, sugar, egg, milk, milk powder (optional), and levain until just combined. Cover and autolyse (rest) for 45 minutes.

Add the salt, and knead on medium-low speed until gluten is moderately developed, about 3 to 5 minutes. The dough will start out sticky and rough but should gradually come together and feel quite smooth and stretchy.

Turn the mixer to low and add the butter in two parts, incorporating the first batch before adding the next. Turn the speed back up to medium-low and continue kneading until the gluten is very well developed and the dough passes the windowpane test, about 10 to 12 minutes. The dough should be smooth and supple.

Shape the dough into a smooth ball and transfer to a clean and lightly oiled container. Cover and let rise at warm room temperature, 78 to 80°F (26 to 27°C) for 2 hours. The dough will be noticeably expanded, but not doubled. At this point, for a same-day bake, continue letting the dough rise until it has increased in size by about 50 percent, about another 1½ to 2 hours; or stretch and fold the dough once (see page 108), cover tightly with plastic wrap, and refrigerate for at least 8 hours and up to 24 hours.

(Continued)

VARIATIONS

Raisin: Add in 100 grams (⅔ cup) of raisins in at the end of mixing.

Matcha: Whisk in 10 grams (1 tbsp plus 2 tsp) of culinary-grade matcha powder in with the flour in the final dough.

Pumpkin: Reduce the milk to 110 grams (½ cup minus 2 tsp) and add 100 grams (½ cup minus 1 tbsp) of pure pumpkin puree in with the wet ingredients.

Whole-Wheat: Use 125 grams (1 cup) of bread flour, 94 grams (¾ cup) of all-purpose flour, and 65 grams (½ cup) of whole-wheat flour in the final dough.

BAKER'S NOTES

For the highest rise and most attractive loaf, I highly recommend using a 9 x 4-inch (23 x 10-cm) Pullman pan. A 9 x 5-inch (23 x 13-cm) loaf pan will work too, though the loaf will be shorter and squatter.

If you want to have this loaf ready to bake in the morning, I suggest building the levain about 36 hours before you want to bake—build the levain the night before mixing, mix the dough in the morning, and shape the loaf, cold from the fridge, right before you go to sleep. It should be ready to bake in the morning. While the crumb of the loaf is slightly more even when the dough is shaped after resting at room temperature, you should still have good results.

Shape and Bake the Loaf: When ready to shape, transfer the dough to a lightly floured surface. Divide the dough into three equal parts and lightly shape each into a ball. Let the dough rest for 10 minutes, if dough has been rising at room temperature, or 45 to 60 minutes, if dough has been refrigerated, covered by lightly oiled plastic. Meanwhile, line a 9 x 4-inch (23 x 10–cm) Pullman pan with parchment paper, leaving 2 to 3 inches (5 to 7.5 cm) of overhang on the long sides for easy removal. Lightly grease the pan and parchment.

Using a lightly floured rolling pin, roll each ball into an oval roughly 8 x 4 inches (20 x 10 cm) (Photo 1). Roll each one up like a jelly roll, starting with a short end (Photos 2 & 3). Let rest for 10 minutes, covered (Photo 4). Roll each piece into an oval again, along the seam (Photo 5), and re-roll as tightly as possible—again, starting with a short end (Photo 6). Transfer the rolls to the prepared pan, seam sides down (Photo 7). Cover loosely with oiled plastic and allow to rise until the dough has roughly tripled in size and fills the pan, about 5 to 6 hours at warm room temperature, 78 to 80°F (26 to 27°C) (Photo 8).

About 45 minutes before baking, preheat the oven to 400°F (200°C) with a rack in the middle. After the dough has finished proofing, lightly brush with milk. Bake at 400°F (200°C) for 20 minutes, then lower the temperature to 350°F (175°C) and bake for another 10 to 15 minutes, or until the loaf sounds hollow when tapped and a digital thermometer registers at least 195°F (91°C) in the center. Tent a piece of foil over the top to keep from overbrowning, if necessary. When the loaf is finished, immediately turn it onto a rack. Brush the melted butter over the top and sides while the loaf is still warm, if desired—this helps keep the crust soft. Allow to cool completely before slicing. Store leftovers in a sealed plastic bag at room temperature for up to 3 days.

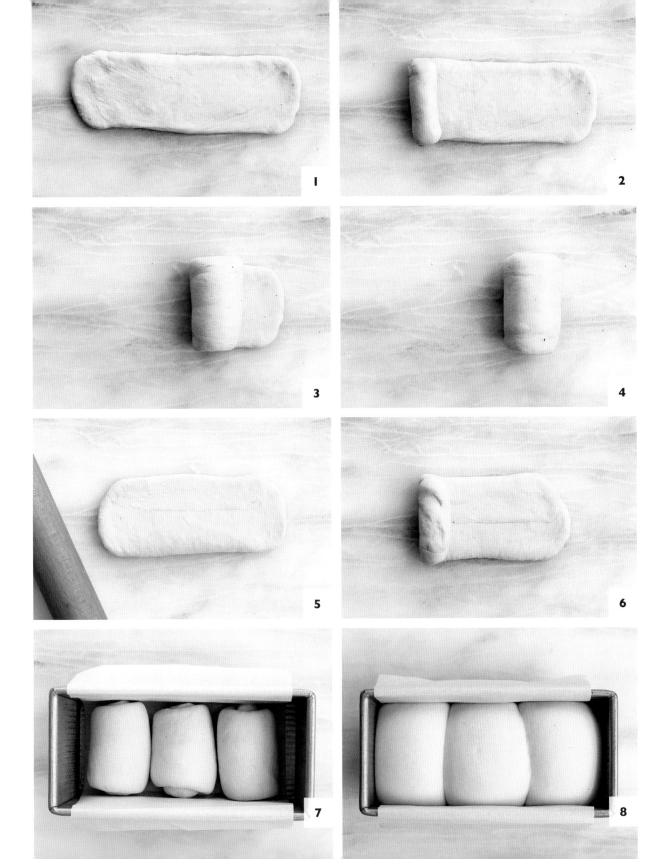

SOURDOUGH CINNAMON ROLLS

LEVAIN
18 g (1 heaping tbsp) ripe sourdough starter (100% hydration)
31 g (2 tbsp) milk
57 g (⅓ cup plus 2 tbsp) bread flour

FINAL DOUGH
125 g (1 cup) bread flour
125 g (1 cup) all-purpose flour
34 g (¼ cup) spelt flour
48 g (4 tbsp) granulated sugar
21 g (3 tbsp) milk powder
1 large egg
104 g (⅓ cup plus 1½ tbsp) milk
88 g (⅓ cup plus 2 tsp) heavy cream
All the levain
7 g (1¾ tsp) kosher salt
45 g (3 tbsp) unsalted butter, at room temperature

FILLING
57 g (¼ cup) unsalted butter, at room temperature
100 g (½ cup) brown sugar (light or dark)
8 g (1 tbsp) ground cinnamon
Pinch of salt

CREAM CHEESE FROSTING
90 g (6 tbsp) cream cheese, at room temperature
56 g (4 tbsp) butter, at room temperature
¾ tsp pure vanilla extract
Pinch of salt
68 g (½ cup plus 1 tbsp) icing sugar

Luscious, swirly cinnamon rolls are my special occasion breakfast of choice—preferably warm, slightly gooey, and generously smeared with cream cheese frosting. For extra flavorful rolls, I use a slightly richer version of my Soft Sourdough Sandwich Bread (page 114) dough as the base. I typically form the rolls right before going to bed; the long proof time means they're ready to be baked when I wake up—the best kind of morning motivation!

Make the Levain: In a medium bowl, mix the starter, milk, and flour together to form a stiff dough. Cover the bowl and ferment the levain at room temperature until more than doubled in volume, puffy, and domed, about 8 to 12 hours.

Mix the Final Dough: In the bowl of a stand mixer fitted with the dough hook, mix together the flours, sugar, milk powder, egg, milk, cream, and levain until just combined. Cover and autolyse (rest) for 45 minutes.

Add the salt and knead on medium-low speed until the gluten is moderately developed, about 5 minutes. The dough will start out sticky and rough but should gradually come together and feel quite smooth and stretchy. Turn the mixer to low and add the butter about 1 tablespoon at a time, incorporating each batch before adding the next. Turn the speed back up to medium-low and continue kneading until the gluten is very well developed and the dough passes the windowpane test, about 10 to 15 minutes. The dough should be smooth and supple.

Shape the dough into a smooth ball and transfer to a lightly oiled container. Cover and let rise at room temperature for 2 hours. The dough will be noticeably expanded but not doubled. Stretch and fold the dough (see page 108), cover, and refrigerate for at least 8 hours and up to 24 hours.

Shape, Proof, and Bake the Rolls: When ready to shape, in a small bowl, cream together the butter, sugar, cinnamon, and salt to form a spreadable paste. Lightly grease a 9 x 9-inch (23 x 23-cm) baking pan or a 9- or 10-inch (23- or 25-cm) round cake pan (preferably aluminum). Take the dough out of the fridge and transfer to a lightly floured surface. Roll into a 14-inch (36-cm) square, doing your best to maintain an even thickness.

Spread the filling mixture evenly over the dough, going all the way to the edges.

Roll the dough up like a jelly roll, pinching to seal. Turn the roll so the seam side is down.

(Continued)

BAKER'S NOTES

For extra gooey rolls, use this trick from Sarah Kieffer of the Vanilla Bean Blog: Spread a small amount of frosting over the rolls as soon as they come out of the oven. Let cool, then spread on the remaining frosting.

These rolls keep well for 2 to 3 days in a sealed plastic bag. Reheat briefly in the microwave to refresh, and wait until just before eating to frost.

Cut into nine even pieces using a sharp knife or unflavored dental floss (my preferred method). Transfer the rolls, cut side up, to the prepared pan, leaving space between each (they will grow into each other during proofing).

Cover the rolls with a piece of lightly oiled plastic wrap. Proof at room temperature, about 74 to 76°F (23 to 24°C), until the dough is very puffy and roughly doubled, about 8 hours or overnight.

About 45 minutes before you're ready to bake, preheat the oven to 400°F (200°C) with a rack in the middle. Bake until the rolls are lightly golden and register 195 to 200°F (91 to 93°C) in the center, about 20 minutes.

Prepare the Cream Cheese Frosting: While the rolls are baking, combine the cream cheese, butter, vanilla, and salt in a medium bowl and beat on medium speed until smooth. Add half of the icing sugar and beat to combine. Add the remaining icing sugar and beat for 1 to 2 minutes, or until fluffy.

Allow the rolls to cool on a wire rack before spreading with frosting (or not; see Baker's Notes). Serve immediately.

VARIATIONS

Cinnamon Swirl Loaf: Omit the butter from the filling and add 8 grams (1 tbsp) of arrowroot or cornstarch. Roll the chilled dough into a 10 x 15–inch (25 x 38–cm) rectangle. Brush the rectangle with an even coat of egg wash (1 large egg, whisked with 1 teaspoon milk or water and a pinch of salt) and sprinkle on about half of the cinnamon-sugar filling mixture over the entire surface. Fold in the long edges so they meet at the middle. You should have a long, skinny rectangle about 15 x 5 inches (38 x 13 cm). Repeat the egg wash and cinnamon-sugar process. Starting with the short end closest to you, roll the rectangle into a tight log. Transfer, seam side down, to a parchment-lined 9 x 5–inch (23 x 13–cm) pan or 9 x 4–inch (23 x 10–cm) Pullman pan. Proof and bake as directed for Soft Sourdough Sandwich Bread (page 114), brushing with the egg wash before baking.

Black Sesame Filling: Reduce the cinnamon in the filling to 1 teaspoon. In a food processor, pulse 18 grams (2 tbsp) of black sesame seeds with the brown sugar until the seeds are finely ground.

Malted: Replace the sugar in the dough with 42 grams (2 tbsp) of barley malt syrup and the milk powder with malted milk powder. Add 9 grams (1 tbsp) of malted milk powder to the filling and 18 grams (2 tbsp) of malted milk powder to the frosting (add with the cream cheese).

Giant Cinnamon Roll: Roll the chilled dough into a 12 x 15–inch (30 x 38–cm) rectangle. Spread with the filling mixture. Using a pizza cutter or sharp knife, cut the dough crosswise into six 2-inch (5-cm) strips. Lightly grease a 9-inch (23-cm) round cake pan. Loosely roll up one strip and place it in the center of the pan. Coil the remaining strips around the middle to form one giant roll. (Don't roll too tightly so the dough has room to expand.) Proof and bake as directed, lowering the temperature to 350°F (175°C) after 20 minutes (the giant roll will take a little longer than individual rolls).

BRAIDED SOURDOUGH CHALLAH

MAKES ONE LARGE BRAID

LEVAIN
40 g (2 heaping tbsp) ripe sourdough starter (100% hydration)

52 g (scant ¼ cup) water, at room temperature

108 g (¾ cup plus 2 tbsp) bread flour

FINAL DOUGH
60 g (¼ cup) warm water

3 large eggs, at room temperature

10 g (2½ tsp) kosher salt

55 g (¼ cup) olive or neutral vegetable oil

65 g (3 tbsp plus 1 tsp) honey or maple syrup

250 g (2 cups) bread flour

100 g (¾ cup plus 2 tsp) all-purpose flour

50 g (⅓ cup plus 1 tbsp) spelt flour

All the levain

TO FINISH
1 large egg, whisked with 1 tsp milk or water and a pinch of salt, for egg wash, divided

Sesame or poppy seeds, or pearl sugar, for garnishing (optional)

With its burnished crust and tender, lightly sweetened crumb, challah is simply a beautiful loaf inside and out. It's also a joy to make—the dough is smooth and easy to handle, perfect for crafting anything from simple swirls to stunning braids. This naturally leavened version makes a generous-sized loaf so you can enjoy it fresh for dinner and still have a few slices left for French toast or Bostock (page 166) in the morning.

Make the Levain: In a medium bowl, mix the starter, water, and flour together to form a stiff dough. Cover the bowl and ferment the levain at room temperature until more than doubled in volume, puffy, and domed, about 8 to 12 hours.

Mix the Final Dough: In the bowl of a stand mixer fitted with the dough hook, whisk together the water, eggs, salt, oil, and honey until combined.

Add the flours and levain (torn into several pieces to make it easier to incorporate). Use a flexible spatula or your hands to mix until all the flour is hydrated and the mixture forms a ball.

Mix the dough on medium-low speed until smooth, about 5 minutes. (You can also knead this dough by hand, which should take 8 to 10 minutes.) The dough should be on the firm side but still easy to knead.

Transfer the dough to a lightly oiled container. Ferment at warm room temperature, 78 to 80°F (26 to 27°C) until doubled, about 4 hours, but timing will depend on the temperature of your kitchen and strength of your starter.

At this point, you can proceed straight to shaping, or stretch and fold the dough as in the directions for Everyday Sourdough Loaf (page 108) and refrigerate for up to 12 hours.

Shape, Proof, and Bake the Loaf: When you are ready to shape, turn the dough out onto a clean work surface (you shouldn't need any flour). Divide the dough equally into thirds. For best results, weigh out the dough into equal portions to ensure an even braid.

Loosely round each piece, then cover and let rest for 10 to 15 minutes. Meanwhile, line a large baking sheet with parchment paper or a silicone mat and prepare the egg wash.

Working with one piece at a time and keeping the rest covered, roll each piece into a thin sheet, about ⅛ inch (3 mm) thick—the shape isn't important, but aim for an even thickness. Roll up tightly like a jelly roll, pinching the seam and ends to seal. Repeat with the other pieces.

(Continued)

Roll each piece into ropes of even lengths—I aim for 16 to 18 inches (41 to 46 cm)—tapering the ends. To form a three-strand braid, position the strands next to each other, seam sides down. Pinch the top ends of the strands together. Lift the left strand and cross it over the middle strand (it will become the new middle strand). Lift the right strand and cross it over the middle strand. Continue all the way down, then pinch the bottom ends together firmly to seal.

Transfer the braided loaf to the prepared baking sheet. Brush the entire surface with a coat of the egg wash, then cover loosely with oiled plastic wrap. Cover and refrigerate the remaining egg wash; you will need it later.

Allow the loaf to proof at room temperature until at least doubled and very puffy (but still defined). If you poke the loaf, the indentation should fill back in very slowly. This takes me about 4 to 5 hours if the dough has not been refrigerated, and closer to 8 hours if it has.

About 45 minutes before baking, preheat the oven to 350°F (175°C) with a rack in the middle. Right after preheating the oven, uncover the loaf and brush with another coat of the egg wash. Keep uncovered while the oven finishes preheating. Right before baking, brush the loaf with a final coat of the egg wash. Sprinkle with seeds or pearl sugar, if using.

Bake for 35 to 45 minutes, rotating the pan halfway through baking, or until the top is well browned and the loaf registers 195°F (91°C) in the center. (Tent with foil if the loaf is browning too quickly.) Cool on a wire rack before slicing. The bread is best served the day it's baked. Store leftovers at room temperature in a sealed plastic bag for up to 3 days.

VARIATIONS

Pumpkin: For a beautiful bronze-hued loaf, replace the 60 grams (¼ cup) of water in the final dough with 75 grams (5 tbsp) of pure pumpkin puree. I like to use maple syrup as the sweetener in this variation.

Raisin: Add 150 grams (1 cup) of raisins to the dough at the end of mixing and before starting the bulk fermentation.

Cinnamon Swirl: Before shaping the dough, mix together 100 grams (½ cup) of light or dark brown sugar and 8 grams (1 tbsp) of ground cinnamon. After rolling each piece into a thin sheet, brush the surface of the dough with the egg wash and sprinkle the filling on top, leaving a ½-inch (1.3-cm) border all around. Roll into logs as directed, taking extra care to seal the seams and ends to prevent the filling from leaking out.

Knots: Divide the dough into fifteen equal portions. Roll each portion into a 12-inch (30-cm) log, then tie a loose knot in the middle. Tuck the left end of the dough up and over the loop and the right side down and under the loop. Press the two ends to secure. Place the shaped rolls on a parchment-lined baking sheet and proof as directed. Bake at 350°F (175°C) for about 20 minutes, or until deeply golden.

BAKER'S NOTES

This recipe is inspired by Maggie Glezer's formula, though I have adjusted the flours and fermentation times.

SAY IT *with* LAYERS: LAMINATED PASTRIES

My ideal weekend starts off with a leisurely cup of coffee and my choice of a buttery, flaky pastry. There's something luxurious about biting into a fresh Danish, hearing that satisfying crunch, and having it flake all over the plate (and your shirt)—the sign of a well-made pastry. Making pastries may sound intimidating, but one of hardest parts is just getting started. You don't need a lot of fancy equipment either—just a good rolling pin and a little elbow grease!

The recipes in this chapter use two versatile doughs: a rough puff pastry dough and a fully laminated Danish dough. The rough puff can be made and used the same day, and is very easy to make. It's the perfect place to start if you're new to laminated doughs. The Danish dough is a two-day process and requires more precision, but it's totally worth it once you see and savor the beautiful buttery layers. Use these doughs to whip up some flaky Morning Buns (page 129) or Spiced Pear Turnovers (page 132) for a fancy breakfast treat; or try the Strawberry Palmiers (page 126) and Spiked Gruyere Twists (page 138) for a sweet-and-savory appetizer spread. Once you see how many beautiful baked goods you can create from a single pastry dough, you won't want to stop!

A NOTE ON BUTTER

While I use American-style butter for most of my baking, I recommend springing for high-quality European-style butter (with at least 82 percent butterfat) when making laminated doughs. Not only will this make your pastries taste especially luxurious, but the lamination process will be easier. In my experience, European-style butter is noticeably more pliable and less prone to breaking due to its lower water content.

STRAWBERRY PALMIERS

MAKES 18–24 COOKIES

ROUGH PUFF PASTRY
250 g (2 cups) all-purpose flour
250 g (2 cups) bread flour
10 g (2½ tsp) kosher salt
35 g (2½ tbsp) granulated sugar
400 g (1¾ cups) cold unsalted
butter (preferably European style),
cut into ½-inch (1.25-cm) cubes
250 g (1 cup plus 2 tsp) cold water

STRAWBERRY SUGAR
(DIVIDED)
15 g (¼ cup) freeze-dried
strawberries
50 g (¼ cup) granulated sugar

TO FINISH
50 g (¼ cup) granulated sugar

If you're looking for a way to spread some love, might I suggest you do it through crisp, buttery cookies? Homemade *palmiers*, to be precise. Traditionally, these French cookies (also known as elephant ears or French hearts) are made by dusting and rolling puff pastry in sugar, then baking until beautifully crisp and caramelized—a simple but addictive treat that goes down perfectly with an espresso or cup of tea. Here, I've jazzed these palmiers up a touch with some freeze-dried strawberries, which add not only a bright flavor but also a pretty naturally pink hue.

Make the Rough Puff Pastry: Whisk together the flours, salt, and sugar in a large bowl.

Add the cold butter to the flour mixture. Use your fingers to flatten the cubes of butter, keeping the pieces of butter fairly large—about the size of walnut halves. Toss with the flour so that all the butter pieces are completely coated.

Add the water and gently stir with a spatula just to combine. The dough should be quite shaggy, but if you squeeze a bit in your hand it should hold together. Cover and chill for 15 to 20 minutes or until cool but not too stiff.

Generously flour a work surface and rolling pin and turn the chilled dough out. Roll the dough into a long rectangle about 8 x 20 inches (20 x 51 cm), roughly ¼ inch (6 mm) thick. The pastry may seem patchy and not cohesive—this is normal; it will come together in the next steps. Try to keep your edges and corners as straight and square as possible, but don't stress too much about it.

Turn the dough so a short side is facing you. Using a bench scraper, fold down the top third and fold up the bottom third as if folding a letter, brushing off excess flour as you fold. Rotate the dough 90 degrees so the opening is on the right. This is your first fold. Wrap the pastry in plastic wrap and chill for 30 minutes.

Repeat the rolling, folding, turning, and chilling three more times for a total of four folds.

After the final fold, wrap the pastry well and chill for at least 45 minutes, or up to 2 days. (For longer storage, freeze well-wrapped dough for up to a month. Thaw overnight in the fridge before using.)

Make the Strawberry Sugar: While the dough is chilling, in the bowl of a food processor, grind the freeze-dried strawberries into a fine powder. Mix with the granulated sugar. Set aside half of the mixture for dipping the finished palmiers.

(Continued)

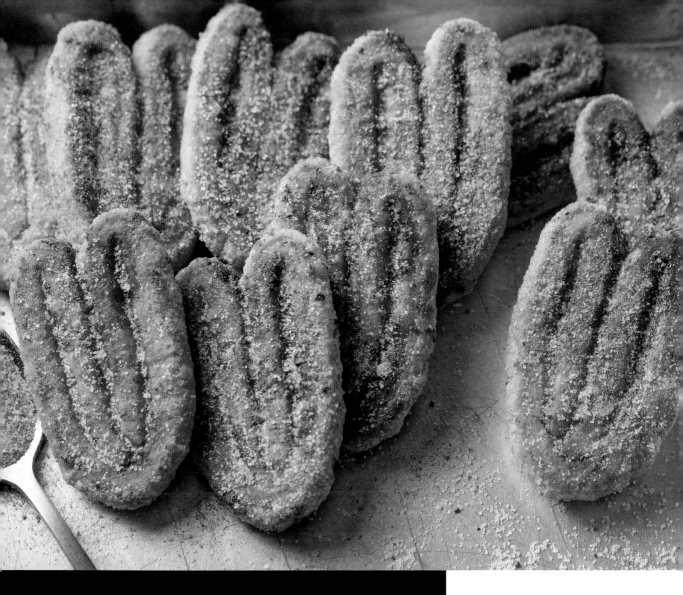

VARIATIONS

Strawberry-Lemon: Grind the zest of 1 lemon with the plain granulated sugar before mixing in the ground freeze-dried strawberries.

Sugar Switch: Replace the strawberry sugar with plain granulated sugar or brown sugar, or a different flavored sugar (page 32).

Savory: Replace the strawberry sugar with ¼ cup (63 g) of prepared pesto or tapenade and sprinkle on 12 grams (2 tbsp) of grated Parmesan before folding. Brush both sides of the log with egg wash (1 large egg, whisked with 1 teaspoon of milk or water and a pinch of salt) before slicing.

BAKER'S NOTES

Depending on the temperature of your kitchen, your pastry may stay cool enough for you to do the first two folds back to back. But don't push it—the butter needs to stay cool for the flaky layers to form in the oven. If at any point the dough starts to feel sticky or warm, wrap and chill it before proceeding.

STRAWBERRY PALMIERS (CONTINUED)

Assemble and Bake the Palmiers: Remove the chilled pastry and cut in half crosswise. Wrap one half of the pastry in plastic wrap and return it to the fridge, or freeze for longer storage. (You'll only need half of the pastry for this recipe.)

On a lightly floured surface, roll the other half of the pastry into a rectangle about 10 x 13 inches (25 x 33 cm), just under ¼ inch (6 mm) thick. Rotate and flip the pastry and flour your surface as needed to avoid sticking. When you've reached the correct size and thickness, use a pastry wheel or a sharp knife to trim the edges to neaten.

Sprinkle an even layer of half of the strawberry-sugar mixture on one side of the dough. Use your rolling pin to gently press the sugar into the dough. Fold the long edges of your pastry in so they meet exactly in the middle, then fold one half over the other half as if closing a book (you'll have a total of four layers). Transfer the log to a baking sheet and chill for about 15 minutes to make cutting the palmiers easier.

While the dough is chilling, preheat the oven to 400°F (200°C) with a rack in the middle and line two baking sheets with parchment paper.

Cut the chilled pastry into ½-inch (1.25-cm)-thick slices. To finish, dip each side in the plain, granulated sugar and place the palmiers on the prepared baking sheets 2 inches (5 cm) apart. (The palmiers will puff significantly in the oven, so leave plenty of space between each.) If the dough is soft at all, return to the fridge or freezer to firm up before baking.

Bake the palmiers, one sheet at a time, for 20 to 30 minutes (keep the remaining unbaked palmiers chilled). Check the bottoms of the palmiers after 10 minutes; if they are brown and caramelized, flip them over for the remaining baking time. If not, keep checking every 1 to 2 minutes until they are. Bake until both sides are a rich golden brown. Transfer to a wire rack to cool. Repeat with the remaining cookies.

Once the palmiers are cool enough to handle, dip each side into the reserved strawberry sugar. Palmiers are best served the day they're baked but will keep for about 5 days at room temperature in an airtight container.

MORNING BUNS

MAKES 12 BUNS

DANISH DOUGH
375 g (3 cups) bread flour

125 g (1 cup) all-purpose flour

38 g (2 tbsp plus 2 tsp) unsalted butter, at room temperature

60 g (¼ cup plus 2 tsp) granulated sugar

10 g (2¼ tsp) kosher salt

7 g (2¼ tsp) instant yeast

120 g (½ cup) water, at room temperature

120 g (½ cup) milk, at room temperature

1 large egg, at room temperature

302 g (1⅓ cups) unsalted butter, cold (for laminating)

Morning buns are basically the love child of a cinnamon roll and a Danish. They're rolled and shaped like cinnamon rolls, but made with laminated dough and dusted with sugar so you get a gorgeously flaky exterior and a soft, caramelized center—textural perfection, in my book. If you're just getting your feet wet with laminated doughs, morning buns are a great place to start as the final dough doesn't have to be rolled too thinly and baking them in a muffin tin helps keep the pastries' shape. And despite their name, morning buns are easily enjoyed any time of the day.

Mix the Dough: In the bowl of a stand mixer fitted with the dough hook, mix together the flours, butter, sugar, salt, yeast, water, milk, and egg until combined, about 5 minutes on low speed. (You can also knead this dough by hand, which will take about 8 to 10 minutes.) The dough doesn't need to be completely smooth (it will gain strength through fermentation and rolling), but it shouldn't be sticky. Flatten into a rough rectangle, place on a baking sheet, wrap with plastic, and refrigerate for at least 8 hours (or up to 15 hours).

Laminate the Dough: About 30 minutes before you want to begin the lamination, take the butter for laminating out of the fridge. Slice into even pieces and pound into an even 8-inch (20-cm) square using a rolling pin. An easy way to do this is to draw an 8-inch (20-cm) square on a piece of parchment, flip it over (so you don't get marker or pencil into your butter), put the butter inside the square, and place another piece of parchment over it. Pound and roll the butter until it is an even square of butter, using a bench scraper to clean up and sharpen the edges and corners as you go. Place the butter back into the fridge to firm up for about 10 to 15 minutes before beginning lamination.

Before you start the lamination, make sure you have a large and clear work surface. You'll also want to have a long rolling pin, measuring tape or ruler, and pastry brush handy, along with a bowl of extra flour for dusting your surface and rolling pin.

Remove the dough from the fridge. On a lightly floured surface, roll the dough into an 8 x 16-inch (20 x 41-cm) rectangle. Remove the butter from the fridge and place it on the bottom half of the dough. Fold the top half of the dough over the bottom half, sandwiching the butter in between. Pinch the edges of the dough around the butter to seal it in.

(Continued)

FILLING AND COATING

165 g (⅓ + ½ cup) granulated sugar, divided, plus more for dusting the tins

65 g (⅓ cup) light brown sugar

8 g (1 tbsp) ground cinnamon

Zest of 1 orange (optional)

Pinch of salt

42 g (3 tbsp) unsalted butter, melted, divided

Turn the dough 90 degrees counter-clockwise so the opening is on the right. Roll the dough into an 8 x 24-inch (20 x 61-cm) rectangle, flouring the dough and rolling pin as necessary. You shouldn't need too much flour, but use as much as you need so nothing sticks. (Just brush off any excess flour with a pastry brush before folding.) Do a single book fold by folding the top third of the dough down and the bottom third up over the middle, using a bit of water to "glue" down the layers. Before folding the top edge down, trim the edge to expose the butter (you can save the scraps and bake them off in a mini loaf pan at the end!). Give the dough a 90-degree clockwise turn so the opening is on the right, cover with plastic, and rest the dough in the fridge for about 20 to 30 minutes.

Do two more book folds following the step above, chilling the dough 20 to 30 minutes after the second fold and at least 90 minutes (or overnight) after the third and final fold. After completing the final fold, the dough can also be well wrapped in plastic wrap and frozen for up to two weeks. Thaw overnight in the fridge before using.

Assemble and Bake the Morning Buns: When you are ready to assemble and bake the buns, mix together 65 grams (⅓ cup) of granulated sugar, the brown sugar, cinnamon, orange zest (if using), and salt in a small bowl and set aside. Prepare a standard 12-cup muffin tin by brushing each cavity with the melted butter (reserving about half) and dusting generously with some of the granulated sugar, tapping out the excess.

Remove the dough from the fridge onto a lightly floured surface. Allow to sit for about 5 to 10 minutes so the butter is pliable. Roll the dough into a large rectangle about 13 x 18 inches (33 x 46 cm), roughly ¼ inch (6 mm) thick. Rotate the dough so a long edge is facing you. Brush the entire surface with the rest of the melted butter, then sprinkle it evenly with the sugar mixture. Use the rolling pin to gently press the sugar into the dough. Starting from the long end closest to you, roll up tightly like a jelly roll. (If the dough is starting to feel soft at this point, chill for about 10 minutes to make cutting easier.) Slice into twelve 1½-inch (4-cm) pieces and place the buns cut side up into the prepared tin. Position the tail ends inward, toward the center of the pan, so that the buns grow into each other and keep from unraveling.

Cover the morning buns with lightly oiled plastic wrap and proof until very puffy and jiggly, about 1½ to 2½ hours at warm room temperature, 78 to 80°F (26 to 27°C). About 30 minutes before baking, preheat the oven to 425°F (220°C) with a rack in the middle.

Bake for 10 minutes, then lower the temperature to 375°F (190°C) and continue baking for another 15 to 20 minutes or until the buns are deeply golden and the centers register at least 200°F (93°C). (If they are browning too quickly, tent with a piece of foil halfway through baking.) Cool the buns in the pan for about 2 minutes, then carefully remove from the tin and roll each bun in the remaining 100 grams (½ cup) of granulated sugar. Morning buns are best consumed the day they're baked, but any extras can be stored in an airtight container and reheated for about 5 minutes at 350°F (175°C) the next day or two.

VARIATIONS

Espresso: Add 4 grams (2 tsp) of espresso powder to the filling ingredients and omit the orange zest. Add another 1 teaspoon of espresso powder to the granulated sugar used to coat the baked morning buns.

Chai-Pecan: Replace the cinnamon in the filling with 1 teaspoon each of ground ginger and ground cinnamon, ½ teaspoon of ground cardamom, ¼ teaspoon each of ground nutmeg and ground allspice, and ⅛ teaspoon of ground cloves. Sprinkle 90 grams (¾ cup) of toasted, chopped pecans on top of the sugar before rolling the dough up.

Berry-Lemon: In place of the granulated and brown sugar in the filling, use 150 grams (¾ cup) of granulated sugar and replace the orange zest with lemon zest. Make a berry sugar for coating the baked morning buns by pulsing together 8 grams (2 tbsp) of freeze-dried strawberries, raspberries, or blueberries with 100 grams (½ cup) of granulated sugar in a food processor.

BAKER'S NOTES

Dough and butter temperature are really important for successful lamination. You want the dough and butter to be similar consistencies so they will roll out easily. The butter should feel cool and pliable—not melty or brittle—and you should be able to bend it without breakage. If the butter is too cold, it will crack into pieces and if it's too warm, it will melt into the dough. I've had best success with a butter temperature around 55 to 60°F (13 to 16°C) at the start of lamination.

SPICED PEAR TURNOVERS

MAKES 8 TURNOVERS

½ batch Rough Puff Pastry
(page 126)

SPICED PEAR FILLING
454 g (3 cups) ripe but firm pears,
peeled and finely diced (about 3
medium pears)
50 g (¼ cup) light brown sugar
Pinch of kosher salt
½ tsp ground cinnamon
½ tsp ground ginger
¼ tsp ground cardamom
¼ tsp ground nutmeg
10 g (2 tsp) lemon juice
½ tsp pure vanilla extract
12 g (1½ tbsp) all-purpose flour
14 g (1 tbsp) unsalted butter

TO FINISH
1 large egg, whisked with 1 tsp milk
or water and a pinch of salt, for egg
wash, divided
Coarse sugar, to taste

Pears often get overshadowed by apples, but they're one of my favorite fruits both for eating and baking. Their delicate flavor pairs well with robust ones such as prosciutto and bleu cheese, but pears have a lovely floral quality that deserves to be enjoyed on its own. These lightly sweetened turnovers make the perfect breakfast on a crisp fall or winter morning.

Make the Spiced Pear Filling: In a medium saucepan, combine the pears, sugar, salt, cinnamon, ginger, cardamom, nutmeg, lemon juice, vanilla, flour, and butter. Stir to combine well. Cook over low heat, stirring frequently, until the pears have softened and the juices are thickened, about 10 minutes. Transfer to a heatproof container and cool to room temperature, then refrigerate until completely chilled.

Assemble and Bake the Turnovers: Preheat the oven to 400°F (200°C) with a rack in the center, and line a large baking sheet with parchment paper.

Roll the puff pastry into a long rectangle a little larger than 8 x 16 inches (20 x 41 cm). Trim the edges to form a neat 8 x 16-inch (20 x 41-cm) rectangle and cut into eight equal squares. Transfer the squares to a plate or baking sheet (it's fine to stack them) and chill for about 10 minutes to relax and firm up the pastry.

Remove the filling and two to three squares of pastry from the fridge (keep the rest of the pastry chilled—I find it's easiest to work with only a few squares at a time). Take one square of pastry and roll it out slightly into a 5-inch (13-cm) square. Brush the edges lightly with the egg wash. Place about 2 tablespoons of the filling in the center of the pastry. Fold the top left corner down to meet the bottom right corner, forming a triangle. Press the edges well to seal, crimping with a fork if desired. Transfer to the prepared baking sheet. Repeat until all the squares have been filled. (You may have some filling leftover, which is excellent over yogurt or ice cream.)

Chill the filled pastries until firm, about 20 to 30 minutes.

Brush the tops of the chilled pastries with the remaining egg wash and prick with a fork or small paring knife to create steam holes. Sprinkle generously with the coarse sugar.

Bake for about 20 to 25 minutes, rotating the sheet halfway through baking, until turnovers are golden brown and puffed. Allow to cool for about 10 to 15 minutes before consuming. Turnovers are best consumed the day they're baked, but any extras can be stored in an airtight container and reheated for about 5 minutes at 350°F (175°C) the next day or two.

VARIATIONS

Cranberry and Cream Cheese: Replace the pear filling with cranberry sauce and Cream Cheese Filling (page 140). Use about 1 tablespoon of each per pastry.

Apple: Replace part, or all, of the pear with the same quantity of peeled, diced baking apples.

Pear and Bacon: Fold in about 56 grams (¼ cup) of chopped bacon bits (cooked and cooled) to the filling right before assembling the pastries.

Berries and Jam: Fill turnovers with about 15 grams (1 tbsp) of thick fruit jam or preserves and a few fresh berries, chopped if large.

BAKER'S NOTES

Firm varieties of pears, such as Bosc and Seckel, work best for baking. Avoid pears that are too ripe or soft.

Unbaked, assembled turnovers freeze well for up to 3 months. Freeze assembled turnovers on a baking sheet, then transfer to a large re-sealable bag for storage. Bake straight from the freezer, egg washing, venting, and sprinkling with sugar right before baking. Frozen pastries may need about 4 to 5 extra minutes of baking time.

Laminated Pastries

SAUSAGE ROLLS *with* FENNEL

**MAKES 32 SMALL
SAUSAGE ROLLS**

**I batch Rough Puff Pastry
(page 126)**

SAUSAGE FILLING
454 g (1 lb) lean ground pork
9 g (2¼ tsp) kosher salt
4 cloves garlic, minced
6 g (2 tsp) fennel seeds, crushed
I tsp coriander seeds, crushed
½ tsp freshly ground black pepper
28 g (¼ cup) breadcrumbs
I large egg
30 g (2 tbsp) heavy cream
15 g (1 tbsp) red wine
A handful of parsley, chopped

TO FINISH
60 g (4 tbsp) Dijon mustard, divided
**I large egg, whisked with 1 tsp milk
or water and a pinch of salt, for egg
wash, divided**
Flaky salt, for garnishing (optional)

Some of my fondest childhood memories involve watching my grandma putter around the kitchen. She would visit us for a few weeks most summers and treat us to her specialties, which included cappuccino cheesecake, Chinese rice dumplings, and sausage rolls. I never got a chance to learn her sausage roll recipe, but I'd like to think she'd approve of these. Juicy, well-seasoned sausage wrapped in crisp, buttery pastry—they really are the perfect bite.

Preheat the oven to 425°F (220°C) with a rack in the center. Line a baking sheet with parchment paper.

In a medium bowl, mix together the pork, salt, garlic, fennel seeds, coriander seeds, pepper, breadcrumbs, egg, cream, wine, and parsley. Refrigerate while you roll out the pastry.

Cut the pastry in half. On a lightly floured surface, roll out each half into a 12-inch (30-cm) square. Cut each square in half for a total of four 6 x 12–inch (15 x 30–cm) pieces.

Spread 15 grams (1 tbsp) of the mustard down the center of each rectangle lengthwise. Divide the sausage mixture into four equal parts and arrange on top of the mustard.

Working one piece at a time, turn the pastry so the sausage mixture is horizontal.

Fold the top of the pastry over the sausage. Brush the bottom part of the pastry with the egg wash and roll the puff pastry with the sausage toward you to seal the roll. Turn the roll so the seam is facing down. Repeat with the remaining pastry.

Refrigerate the assembled rolls for about 20 minutes, or until pastry is firm.

Using a sharp knife, cut each chilled roll into eight pieces. Arrange the sausage rolls, seam side down on the prepared baking sheet about 1 inch (2.5 cm) apart.

Brush the pastry with the remaining egg wash, followed by a pinch of flaky salt, if desired.

Bake for 20 to 30 minutes, rotating halfway through, or until the pastry is golden brown and the sausage is cooked through. Serve warm or at room temperature. Refrigerate leftovers in an airtight container for up to 3 days.

VARIATIONS

Turkey Breakfast Sausage: In the sausage filling, omit the cream, red wine, and parsley. Replace the ground pork with 454 grams (1 lb) of ground turkey. Reduce the garlic to 2 cloves. Replace the fennel and coriander seeds with ¼ teaspoon each of dried tarragon and sage. Add 40 grams (2 tbsp) of maple syrup, 8 grams (2 tsp) of granulated sugar, and 75 grams (½ cup) of fresh blueberries. Omit the Dijon mustard when assembling the rolls.

Goat Cheese and Cranberry: In the sausage filling, omit the cream. Add 60 grams (¼ cup) of goat cheese and 60 grams (½ cup) of chopped, dried cranberries. Omit the Dijon mustard when assembling the rolls.

Chorizo: In the sausage filling, omit the fennel seeds, coriander seeds, and black pepper. Add 2 tablespoons of paprika, 1 tablespoon each of dried oregano and ground cumin, and ¼ teaspoon each of ground cinnamon, allspice, and cloves. For a spicy version, add ½ teaspoon of cayenne pepper (or to taste). Omit the Dijon mustard when assembling the rolls.

BAKER'S NOTES

You can cut the rolls into larger pieces, increasing bake time as needed. For sausage rolls longer than 2 inches (5 cm), cut two steam vents on top before baking.

Unbaked, assembled sausage rolls freeze well for up to 3 months. Freeze assembled sausage rolls (cut to desired size) on a baking sheet, then transfer to a large re-sealable bag for storage. Bake straight from the freezer, egg washing, venting, and sprinkling with salt right before baking. Frozen sausage rolls may need about 4 to 5 extra minutes of baking time.

CURRY BEEF PUFFS

MAKES SIXTEEN 3–INCH
(7.5–CM) PUFFS

½ batch Rough Puff Pastry
(page 126)

CURRY BEEF FILLING
15 g (1 tbsp) vegetable oil
½ medium onion, finely diced
3 cloves garlic, minced
2–3 slices fresh ginger
Soy sauce, to taste
Sugar, to taste
225 g (½ lb) lean ground beef
½ medium carrot, shredded
16 g (1 tbsp) curry paste, or 6 g
(1 tbsp) curry powder, or 30 g
(1 block) curry roux
60 g (¼ cup) water, plus more as
needed
Salt and pepper, to taste

TO FINISH
1 large egg, whisked with 1 tsp milk
or water and a pinch of salt, for egg
wash, divided
Sesame seeds, for garnishing
(optional)

Curry beef puffs are a popular item in traditional Chinese bakeries, a welcome savory item among all the sweet offerings. The best curry puffs are packed with an intensely flavored filling of ground beef and vegetables. While you can use plain curry powder, I prefer the flavor of either Hong Kong–style curry paste or a block of curry roux, both of which are readily available at Asian supermarkets or online suppliers.

Make the Curry Beef Filling: Heat the oil in a medium saucepan over medium-high heat. When the oil is hot, add the onion, garlic, and ginger. Season with a little of the soy sauce and sugar, and sauté until the onion is softened, about 3 to 5 minutes. Add the ground beef, using a wooden spoon or spatula to break up the meat. Cook until the beef is no longer pink, stirring frequently.

Add the carrot, curry paste, and water. Stir to combine. Bring to a boil, then turn down the heat to low. Simmer uncovered, stirring occasionally, until the onions are completely soft and the mixture is thick, about 30 minutes. If the mixture starts to look dry or the onions don't seem to be breaking down, add 1 tablespoon of water. I usually add about 2 tablespoons more water during the simmering process.

Turn off the heat and check for seasonings, adding salt, sugar, and pepper to taste. The filling should be just on the edge of over-seasoned in order to cut through the rich pastry. Cool to room temperature, remove the ginger slices, then cover and refrigerate until cold.

Assemble and Bake the Puffs: Preheat the oven to 400°F (200°C) with a rack in the center. Line two baking sheets with parchment paper.

On a lightly floured surface, roll the puff pastry slightly larger than 12-inch (30-cm) square, just under ¼ inch (6 mm) thick. Trim the edges to form a neat 12-inch (30-cm) square, then cut the sheet into sixteen 3-inch (7.5-cm) squares. Transfer the squares to a plate or baking sheet (it's fine to stack them) and chill for about 10 minutes to relax and firm up the pastry.

Remove the filling and two to three squares of pastry from the fridge, leaving the rest chilled. Brush the edges of one square with the egg wash. Place 1 heaping teaspoon of the filling in the center of the pastry. Fold the top left corner down to meet the bottom right corner, forming a triangle. Press the edges to seal, then use a fork to crimp the edges. Transfer to the prepared baking sheets, spacing the puffs about 1 inch (2.5 cm) apart. Repeat until all the squares have been filled. Avoid the temptation to overfill the pastries, or else they tend to burst in the oven. (You may have some filling leftover, which you can freeze for future pastries or enjoy over rice or noodles.) Chill the filled pastries until firm, about 20 to 30 minutes.

Brush the tops of the chilled pastries with the remaining egg wash and prick with a fork to create steam holes. Sprinkle with sesame seeds, if using. Bake the sheets one at a time for about 20 to 25 minutes, rotating halfway through baking, or until pastries are golden brown and puffed. Allow to cool for about 10 to 15 minutes before consuming.

VARIATIONS

Extra-Large Puffs: Cut the pastry into nine equal squares instead of sixteen. Fill each with 1 heaping tablespoon of the filling. Larger puffs may need about 3 or 4 extra minutes to bake.

Chicken Pie Puffs: Replace the Curry Beef Filling with half of the chicken pot pie filling (page 63), chilled.

Potato and Peas: Replace the ground beef with 227 grams (½ lb) of Yukon Gold potatoes, peeled and diced into ½-inch (1.3-cm) cubes. Add the potato with the carrot and curry paste. Once the potato is soft, add 63 grams (½ cup) of frozen peas and cook just until the peas are warmed through.

BAKER'S NOTES

Unbaked, assembled puffs freeze well for up to 3 months. Freeze assembled puffs on a baking sheet, then transfer to a large re-sealable bag for storage. Bake straight from the freezer, egg washing, venting, and sprinkling with sesame seeds (if using) right before baking. Frozen puffs may need about 4 to 5 extra minutes of baking time.

Laminated Pastries   137

SPIKED GRUYERE TWISTS

MAKES ABOUT
24 TWISTS

½ batch Rough Puff Pastry
(page 126)

CHEESE SPRINKLE
113 g (1 cup) grated aged Gruyere
cheese
50 g (½ cup) grated Parmesan
cheese
½ tsp cayenne pepper
½ tsp ground mustard
¼ tsp kosher salt
Freshly ground black pepper, to
taste

TO FINISH
1 large egg, whisked with 1 tsp milk
or water and a pinch of salt, for egg
wash

These flaky, crunchy, cheesy twists are one of the simplest things you can make with puff pastry. They make a perfect appetizer or party snack—set them out in a jar and just watch them disappear!

Line two baking sheets with parchment paper. In a medium bowl, mix together the cheeses, cayenne, mustard, salt, and pepper.

On a lightly floured surface, roll the pastry into a rectangle about 12 x 16 inches (30 x 41 cm). Brush the entire surface of the pastry with the egg wash and sprinkle the cheese mixture evenly over the top. Use a rolling pin to press lightly down on the cheese to adhere.

Cut the pastry in half crosswise so you have two pieces about 12 x 8 inches (30 x 20 cm). Stack one piece of pastry on top of the other, cheese sides up. Roll the stacked pastry into a 12-inch (30-cm) square.

Using a sharp knife or pizza cutter, cut the pastry into ½-inch (1.3-cm) strips. Take one strip and twist the two ends in opposite directions several times. Transfer to a prepared sheet tray and press the ends firmly down onto the parchment (this helps the twists keep their shape). Repeat with the remaining strips, spacing them on the prepared baking sheets about 1 inch (2.5 cm) apart.

Chill until the pastry is firm, about 30 to 60 minutes. Meanwhile, preheat the oven to 400°F (200°C) with a rack in the middle.

Bake the sheets one at a time for about 25 to 30 minutes, or until the pastry is well browned and crisp (keep the second sheet chilled). For even browning, use a pair of tongs to flip the twists over about halfway through baking, or once they are set enough to handle. Transfer the sheets to a wire rack to cool completely before serving. The twists are best served the day they're made, but leftovers will keep in an airtight container at room temperature for up to 3 days.

VARIATIONS

Seeded: For extra crunch, sprinkle about 18 grams (2 tbsp) of poppy or sesame seeds on top of the puff pastry after the cheese.

Garlic-Herb: Mix 1 teaspoon of garlic powder and about 3 to 4 tablespoons of freshly minced herbs (such as parsley, thyme, oregano, chives, or basil) or 2 to 3 teaspoons of dried herbs in with the cheese mixture before sprinkling on the puff pastry.

Cinnamon-Sugar: Omit the cheese and spices. In a small bowl, mix together 50 grams (¼ cup) each of granulated sugar and brown sugar and 8 grams (1 tbsp) of ground cinnamon. Sprinkle about half of the mixture over each piece of puff pastry after the egg wash.

BAKER'S NOTES

Unbaked twists freeze well for up to 3 months. Freeze the assembled twists on a baking sheet, then transfer to a large re-sealable bag for storage. Bake straight from the freezer— frozen twists may need about 3 or 4 extra minutes of baking time.

LEMON–CREAM CHEESE DANISH BRAID

MAKES ONE LARGE BRAID

½ batch Danish pastry dough
(page 129)

CREAM CHEESE FILLING
125 g (½ block) cream cheese,
softened

28 g (2 tbsp) granulated sugar

½ tsp pure vanilla extract

¼ tsp kosher salt

I tsp lemon juice, or to taste

TO ASSEMBLE
85 g (⅓ cup) Meyer Lemon Curd
(page 79) or plain lemon curd

I large egg, whisked with I tsp milk
or water and a pinch of salt, for egg
wash

Coarse or pearl sugar, for sprinkling
(optional)

SIMPLE SYRUP
50 g (¼ cup) granulated sugar

60 g (¼ cup) water

SOUR CREAM GLAZE
90 g (¾ cup) icing sugar, sifted

22 g (1½ tbsp) sour cream

Pinch of salt

Milk or water, as needed

This beautiful Danish braid makes a stunning centerpiece for brunch or a holiday celebration. The tangy, creamy lemon curd and cream cheese filling holds its own against the rich, buttery pastry, and a simple plaiting technique makes this shareable treat look as if it came straight from an artisan bakery. For extra shine and sparkle, brush the freshly baked braid with simple syrup and finish with a generous drizzle of sour cream glaze.

Make the Cream Cheese Filling: In a small bowl, cream together the cream cheese, sugar, vanilla, salt, and lemon juice until smooth. Taste and add more lemon juice if desired. (The filling can be made up to 3 days in advance and refrigerated; bring to room temperature before using.)

Assemble and Bake the Danish: On a lightly floured surface, roll the pastry into a large rectangle about 9½ x 14 inches (24 x 36 cm). Transfer the dough to a large piece of parchment paper.

Spread the cream cheese filling in an even strip down the center of the rectangle lengthwise, about 1½ to 1¾ inches (3.8 to 4 cm) wide, leaving a ½-inch (1.3-cm) space on the top and bottom. Spoon the lemon curd evenly on top of the cream cheese (Photo 1, page 142). While it's tempting to want to stuff the braid full, don't go overboard or the filling may burst out the sides and mar the look of the final braid. Use a sharp knife or bench scraper to cut ½-inch (1.3-cm) crosswise strips down the length of the rectangle on both sides of the filling, ensuring you have the same number of strips on each side (Photo 2, page 142).

Starting at the top, fold the left dough strip at a slight diagonal over the filling. Repeat on the other side, so the two strips are crisscrossed over the filling (Photo 3, page 142). Repeat all the way down the rectangle (Photo 4, page 142). When you get to the bottom, tuck the ends of the last two strips under the braid. Stack two large baking sheets together and transfer the braid, still on the parchment, to the top sheet. (This keeps the bottoms from scorching during baking.)

Brush the braid lightly with the egg wash and cover loosely with lightly oiled plastic. Cover and refrigerate the remaining egg wash; you will need it later. Proof the braid at warm room temperature, 78 to 80°F (26 to 27°C), for about 1½ to 2½ hours, or until the braid is very puffy and the layers are clearly visible.

While the pastry is proofing, make the simple syrup. Combine the sugar and water in a small saucepan. Bring to a simmer over medium heat, stirring occasionally. Once the sugar is dissolved, remove from the heat, and pour into a heat-safe jar.

(Continued)

VARIATIONS

Puff Pastry: Use this same shaping technique with ½ batch of Rough Puff Pastry (page 126). Chill the shaped braid until firm, then bake at 400°F (200°C) until deeply golden brown and puffed, about 25 to 30 minutes.

Pear-Almond: Replace the cream cheese filling with frangipane (page 166). Replace the lemon curd with ½ batch of Spiced Pear Filling (page 132). After glazing, sprinkle the finished braid with sliced almonds.

Other Fruit Fillings: Replace the lemon curd with an equal amount of fruit jam, such as raspberry (page 76) or rhubarb (page 42), fruit preserves, or fruit butter. You can also use about 1 cup of fresh berries, chopped if large. I recommend raspberries, blueberries, and/or blackberries—avoid strawberries as they tend to be too wet.

LEMON–CREAM CHEESE DANISH BREAD (CONTINUED)

About 45 minutes before baking, preheat the oven to 400°F (200°C) with a rack in the middle. Right before baking, brush the braid with a second coat of the egg wash. Sprinkle with coarse or pearl sugar, if using.

Bake for 10 minutes, then turn the heat down to 375°F (190°C) and continue baking for another 20 to 25 minutes or until the braid is deeply golden.

As soon as the braid is out of the oven, brush with the simple syrup. Cool on a wire rack for about 15 minutes before glazing.

Make the Sour Cream Glaze: When ready to glaze, sift the icing sugar into a small bowl. Add the sour cream and salt and whisk thoroughly to combine. Add the milk or water 1 teaspoon at a time, whisking well after each addition, until the desired glaze consistency is reached. Use a spoon to drizzle the glaze over the braid. Allow the glaze to set for about 10 minutes before serving. The Danish is best served the day it is baked.

MUSHROOM DIAMOND PASTRIES

½ batch Danish pastry dough
(page 129)

MUSHROOM FILLING
30 g (2 tbsp) olive oil

1 shallot, diced

454 g (1 lb) variety of fresh
mushrooms, finely sliced

½ tsp dried thyme

Salt and pepper, to taste

15 g (1 tbsp) red wine vinegar

TO FINISH
1 large egg, whisked with 1 tsp milk
or water and a pinch of salt, for egg
wash, divided

30 g (6 tsp) Dijon mustard, divided

Flaky salt, for sprinkling

Chopped parsley or chives, for
garnish (optional)

These savory Danishes were inspired by one of the most memorable dishes I ever ordered—a simple soup that was just loads of mushrooms cooked down in batches. It was an intensely umami-packed bowl with no need for cheese, cream, or bacon to enhance the flavor. That refreshingly pure soup was a good reminder that simple, quality ingredients often don't need much help to shine. For these savory pastries, try to use a variety of fresh mushrooms for the filling—then make them for the mushroom lovers in your life.

Make the Mushroom Filling: In a medium skillet over medium heat, heat the oil until shimmering. Sauté the shallot until translucent, about 3 minutes. Add the mushrooms and thyme. Season with salt and pepper and sauté until the mushrooms have released all their liquid. Continue cooking over medium heat, stirring occasionally, until the liquid has evaporated completely, about 30 minutes. Stir in the red wine vinegar and continue cooking until evaporated. Remove from the heat. Taste and adjust the seasonings. Cool to room temperature before filling the pastries.

Shape, Assemble, and Bake the Pastries: On a lightly floured surface, roll the Danish dough into a large rectangle about 10 x 14 inches (25 x 36 cm). Trim the edges so you have a neat rectangle measuring 9 x 13½ inches (23 x 34 cm). Cut the dough into six 4½-inch (11-cm) squares. Stack, cover with plastic wrap, and refrigerate for about 10 minutes to relax the gluten.

Stack two large baking sheets together and line the top one with parchment paper. (This keeps the bottoms from scorching during baking.) Remove one square of pastry from the fridge, keeping the rest chilled (Photo 1, page 144). To shape into a diamond, gently fold the pastry square on the diagonal to form a triangle, making sure the corners line up (Photo 2, page 144). Using a sharp knife, make two cuts parallel to the sides of the triangle, leaving about ¼ inch (6 mm) of pastry on the edges (Photo 3, page 144). Don't let the cuts meet or you will end up with two pieces of pastry! Unfold the dough and orient the square so it is like a diamond (Photo 4, page 144). Fold one edge over so it meets the cut you just made (Photo 5, page 144). Repeat with the other edge to form a diamond (Photo 6, page 144).

Repeat with the remaining squares and transfer to the prepared baking sheet, spacing the squares about 2 inches (5 cm) apart.

Brush the shaped pastries with the egg wash and cover loosely with lightly oiled plastic wrap. Cover and refrigerate the remaining egg wash; you will need it later. Place the pastries in a warm area to proof until doubled in size and layers are very visible—about 1½ to 2½ hours.

(Continued)

MUSHROOM DIAMOND PASTRIES (CONTINUED)

When the pastries are nearly finished proofing, preheat the oven to 425°F (220°C) with a rack in the middle. Right before baking, spread 1 teaspoon of the mustard over the center of the pastry. Spoon the mushroom filling on top of the mustard, about 2 tablespoons per pastry. Brush the edges of the pastry with another coat of the egg wash and sprinkle with flaky salt.

Bake at 425°F (220°C) for 10 minutes, then lower the temperature to 375°F (190°C) and bake for another 10 to 20 minutes, or until well risen and browned. Cool on a wire rack for about 10 minutes before serving. Garnish with chopped herbs, if using, right before serving. The pastries are best served the day they're baked.

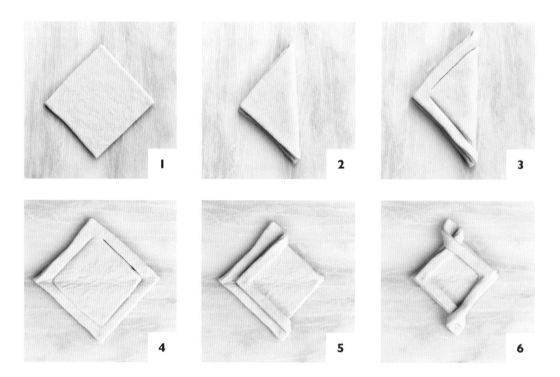

VARIATIONS

Asparagus, Prosciutto, and Goat Cheese: Right before baking, spread about 15 grams (1 tbsp) of soft goat cheese in the center of each Danish. Cut eight medium-thin asparagus stalks into 1-inch (2.5-cm) pieces and toss with a dash of olive oil, salt, and pepper. Sprinkle the asparagus pieces evenly over the goat cheese. Cut six slices of prosciutto into thin strips and sprinkle evenly over the asparagus. Bake as directed.

Fruit and Cream Cheese: Right before baking, fill the center of the pastries with 1 to 2 tablespoons of Cream Cheese Filling (page 140). Top with two or three slices of fresh peaches or two fig halves, cut side up, or a small spoonful of thick fruit preserves. Bake as directed, omitting the flaky salt. Brush the baked pastries with Simple Syrup (page 140), if desired.

Pocket Shape: This popular Danish shape is very simple and works well for any kind of filling that isn't too runny. After cutting the pastry into squares, dab a little egg wash on the corners of each square. Fold each corner into the center and press down gently. Proof as directed. Fill the Danishes right before baking, spooning or piping the filling into the center (if the corners have popped open during proofing, press them back down before filling). Bake as directed.

BAKER'S NOTES

Danish dough proofs best in a warm, humid environment. The oven with the light on and a pan of warm water on the shelf below the Danishes is a great proofing spot. Don't let the temperature get above 80°F (27°C), though, or the butter will leak out of the pastries.

PAINS AUX RAISINS

½ batch Danish pastry dough
(page 129)
120 g (½ cup) Vanilla-Almond
Pastry Cream (page 162) or
frangipane (page 166) (see Baker's
Notes)
100 g (⅔ cup) raisins, soaked in hot
water for 1 hour and drained
1 large egg, whisked with 1 tsp milk
or water and a pinch of salt, for egg
wash, divided

SIMPLE SYRUP
100 g (½ cup) granulated sugar
120 g (½ cup) water

If I lived in Paris, there's a strong possibility that I'd start each morning with coffee and a *pain aux raisins*, a swirl-shaped pastry made with laminated dough and stuffed with plump, juicy raisins. Pains aux raisins are not quite as common in bakeries here in Canada, so naturally, I had to learn to make my own. Biting into one still warm from the oven, the buttery aroma filling the air, may not quite transport me to a Parisian café—but it does fill me with a *joie de vivre*.

Stack two large baking sheets together and line the top one with parchment paper. (This keeps the bottoms from scorching during baking.)

On a lightly floured surface, roll the pastry into a rectangle about 10 x 15 inches (25 x 38 cm), just under ¼ inch (6 mm) thick. Trim the edges to neaten. Spread a thin layer of the pastry cream or frangipane over the entire surface. Scatter the raisins evenly on top. Starting with the short end closest to you, roll the pastry up like a jelly roll. (If the dough is starting to feel soft at this point, chill for about 10 minutes to make cutting easier.) Slice into eight even pieces, about 1¼ inch (3 cm) thick, and place the pastries, cut side up, on the prepared baking sheet at least 2½ inches (6 cm) apart. Tuck the tail of each roll underneath so the spirals don't unravel.

Brush the pastries with the egg wash and cover with lightly oiled plastic wrap. Cover and refrigerate the remaining egg wash; you will need it later.

Proof until very puffy and jiggly, about 2 to 3 hours at warm room temperature, 78 to 80°F (26 to 27°C).

While the pastries are proofing, make the simple syrup. Combine the sugar and water in a small saucepan. Bring to a simmer over medium heat, stirring occasionally. Once the sugar is dissolved, remove from the heat and pour into a heat-safe jar.

About 30 minutes before baking, preheat the oven to 425°F (220°C) with a rack in the middle.

Brush the proofed pastries with a second coat of the egg wash. Bake for 10 minutes, then lower the temperature to 375°F (190°C) and continue baking for another 15 to 20 minutes or until the pastries are deeply golden. Rotate the pan about halfway through baking. Remove from the oven and brush the pastries with Simple Syrup. (Pour out a small quantity of the syrup to use for the pastries to keep from getting crumbs in the entire batch—the rest can be refrigerated indefinitely.) Cool on a wire rack briefly before devouring. The pastries are best consumed the day they're baked, but any extras can be stored in an airtight container and reheated for about 5 minutes at 350°F (175°C) the next day or two.

VARIATIONS

Cherry-Pistachio: Make the frangipane (page 166) with finely ground pistachios in place of the almond flour. Replace the raisins with chopped dried cherries. After brushing the finished Danishes with the syrup, sprinkle with finely chopped pistachios.

Pesto: Replace the Vanilla-Almond Pastry Cream (page 162) or frangipane (page 166) and raisins with 100 grams (scant ½ cup) of pesto and 25 grams (¼ cup) of grated hard cheese. Omit the Simple Syrup glaze.

Apple: Peel and finely dice one large baking apple. Melt about 14 grams (1 tbsp) of butter in a medium saucepan and add the apple, 25 grams (2 tbsp) of brown sugar, a pinch of salt, ½ teaspoon of ground cinnamon, and a squeeze of lemon juice. Sauté until the apple is soft, then add 50 grams (⅓ cup) of raisins, if desired. Cool completely, then spread over the pastry cream or frangipane.

BAKER'S NOTES

Pastry cream is the traditional filling for these pastries. However, since you only need a small amount of filling—just enough to stick the raisins down—using frangipane is more practical for the home kitchen. It's quicker to make, and leftovers can be frozen. If you have pastry cream left over from another project, feel free to use it in place of the frangipane.

PUFFED PERFECTION: PÂTE À CHOUX

Pâte à choux is a light and airy dough that is the foundation for many pastries. Everything from simple Birthday Profiteroles (page 152) to sky-high croquembouches start with this incredibly versatile classic French pastry batter. And good news—it's not difficult to make at home.

Pâte à choux starts with very basic ingredients: flour, water and/or milk, butter, and a touch of salt and sugar. The process of making pâte à choux is a little unusual. First, you cook a paste on the stovetop before adding eggs to make a smooth and shiny dough. After being shaped, the pastry is cooked a second time in the oven (or in hot oil). This is where the magic happens: If made properly, the heat will cause the high moisture content of the dough to create steam. The evaporating steam causes the pastries to puff up, leaving behind light and airy hollow shells.

Because pâte à choux dough is barely sweetened, it shines in both sweet and savory applications. From cheesy Smoked Paprika and Cheddar Gougères (page 150) to Lime Cheesecake Éclairs (page 155) to fried Maple-Glazed Crullers (page 158)—and with multiple variations for each—there's a recipe in this chapter for whatever you're craving. I hope they will inspire you to master this do-it-all dough and fill it with whatever tickles your fancy.

SMOKED PAPRIKA *and* CHEDDAR GOUGÈRES

**MAKES ABOUT
15 GOUGÈRES**

75 g (⅓ cup minus 1 tsp) water

75 g (⅓ cup minus 1 tsp) milk

57 g (¼ cup) unsalted butter, cubed

1 tsp granulated sugar

½ tsp kosher salt

½ tsp smoked paprika

½ tsp mustard powder

Several turns of freshly ground black pepper

100 g (¾ cup plus 2 tsp) all-purpose or bread flour, sifted (see Baker's Notes)

150 g eggs (about 3 large), at room temperature and lightly beaten to combine

100 g (scant 1 cup) grated aged cheddar cheese, divided

12 g (¼ cup) finely chopped chives or scallions

We all need a few back-pocket recipes that are good for crowds, easy to prepare, and delightfully delicious. *Gougères*, or French cheese puffs, fit the bill perfectly. They are made with the classic pâte à choux dough; but before baking, you mix in some cheese to make savory little appetizers that go down *just* right with a glass of wine.

Preheat the oven to 375°F (190°C) with a rack in the middle and line a large baking sheet with parchment paper.

Combine the water, milk, butter, sugar, salt, paprika, mustard, and pepper in a medium saucepan. Bring to a strong simmer over medium heat, stirring occasionally. As soon as the mixture is simmering, remove the pot from the heat and dump the flour in all at once. Stir vigorously with a wooden spoon or spatula until the flour is completely incorporated.

Return the pot to low heat. Continue stirring vigorously until the mixture clears the side of the pot and forms a ball and a thin film forms on the bottom of the pot, about 2 to 3 minutes. The dough should be stiff enough that if you stick a small spoon in it, the spoon remains upright. Immediately transfer the dough to the bowl of a stand mixer fitted with the paddle attachment.

Mix the dough on low speed for 1 to 2 minutes to release the steam. An instant-read thermometer should read no warmer than 140°F (60°C).

When the dough has cooled sufficiently and with the mixer still on low, add about half of the beaten eggs in a slow, steady stream. Turn up the speed to medium and mix until the egg has been completely absorbed. Add more egg about 1 tablespoon at a time, mixing each addition in completely before adding more. When you've added most of the egg and the dough has taken on a glossy sheen, check the dough consistency—a finger dragged through it should leave a trough and a peak of dough should form where the finger is lifted. Once the dough passes this test, it's ready. You may not need all the egg—I usually have 1 to 2 tablespoons left over.

Set aside about one quarter of the cheese. Add the remaining cheese and the chives to the dough and use a flexible spatula to combine. Using a cookie scoop or a piping bag fitted with a large round tip, portion the dough into about 15 golf ball–sized mounds onto the prepared sheet, leaving about 2 inches (5 cm) between each. Sprinkle the tops of the gougères with the reserved cheese.

Bake the gougères for about 30 to 40 minutes, or until they are completely golden brown and feel light when you pick one up. (Avoid opening the oven for the first 25 minutes of baking or the gougères may collapse.) When the gougères are done, turn the oven off, prop open the door, and cool the gougères in the oven for about 5 to 10 minutes.

Gougères are best served still slightly warm, but they can be made a day ahead and reheated in a 300°F (150°C) oven for 5 to 10 minutes before serving.

VARIATIONS

Cheese Swap: Substitute the Cheddar cheese with another strong cheese or mix of cheeses, such as Gruyère, Parmesan, or Comté. Choose cheeses that are low in moisture so the dough doesn't become too wet.

Bacon: Mix in about 100 grams (½ cup) of bacon bits (cooked and cooled) with the cheese and chives.

Jumbo or Mini Gougères: You can shape gougères into ice-cream-scoop-sized or bite-size portions—just keep the gougères on each sheet a consistent size so they bake evenly. Larger gougères will take 2 to 3 extra minutes to bake and smaller ones 2 to 3 minutes less.

BAKER'S NOTES

You can use either all-purpose flour or bread flour for gougères. All-purpose flour yields softer puffs, while bread flour makes them rounder and sturdier.

For extra crisp puffs, use a skewer or paring knife to poke a hole in the side of each gougère for the last 5 minutes of baking.

BIRTHDAY PROFITEROLES

MAKES ABOUT
15–20 PROFITEROLES

CHOUX PASTRY
75 g (⅓ cup minus 1 tsp) water
75 g (⅓ cup minus 1 tsp) milk
70 g (5 tbsp) unsalted butter
1 tsp granulated sugar
½ tsp kosher salt
100 g (¾ cup plus 2 tsp) all-purpose
flour, sifted
150 g eggs (about 3 large), at room
temperature and lightly beaten to
combine
1 large egg, whisked with 1 tsp milk
or water and a pinch of salt, for egg
wash

Birthdays during my childhood were typically celebrated not with cake, but with a box of ice cream decorated to the nines with candy and sprinkles. This dessert combines those sweet memories with classic *profiteroles*: plain vanilla ice cream gets the birthday treatment with the addition of cake crumbs and sprinkles and is scooped into *choux* shells. Add a drizzle of hot fudge sauce and another handful of sprinkles, and you've got yourself a party.

Make the Choux Pastry: Preheat the oven to 375°F (190°C) with a rack in the middle and line a large baking sheet with parchment paper.

Combine the water, milk, butter, sugar, and salt in a medium saucepan. Bring to a strong simmer over medium heat, stirring occasionally. As soon as the mixture is simmering, remove the pot from the heat and dump the flour in all at once. Stir vigorously with a wooden spoon or spatula until the flour is completely incorporated.

Return the pot to low heat. Continue stirring vigorously until the mixture clears the side of the pot and forms a ball and a thin film forms on the bottom of the pot, about 2 to 3 minutes. The dough should be stiff enough that if you stick a small spoon in it, the spoon remains upright. Immediately transfer the dough to the bowl of a stand mixer fitted with the paddle attachment.

Mix the dough on low speed for 1 to 2 minutes to release the steam. An instant-read thermometer should read no warmer than 140°F (60°C)—any hotter and you'll cook the eggs when adding them!

When the dough has cooled sufficiently and with the mixer still on low, add about one-third of the beaten eggs in a slow, steady stream. Mix until the egg has been completely absorbed, then add more egg 1 tablespoon at a time, mixing each addition in completely before adding more. When you've added most of the egg and the dough has taken on a glossy sheen, check the dough consistency—a finger dragged through it should leave a trough and a peak of dough should form where the finger is lifted. Once the dough passes this test, it's ready. You may not need all the egg—I usually have 1 to 2 tablespoons left over.

Transfer the dough to a piping bag fitted with a large round piping tip. Pipe mounds of dough about 1½ inches (4 cm) in diameter on the prepared baking sheet, leaving about 2 inches (5 cm) between each. Use a wet finger to pat down any peaks on the buns to keep them from scorching in the oven. Brush the tops lightly with the egg wash.

Bake for about 30 to 40 minutes, or until the puffs are completely golden brown and feel hollow when you pick one up. About 5 minutes before the puffs are done, use a skewer or small knife to poke a small hole in each puff to help them crisp. Once the puffs are done, turn the oven off, prop open the door, and allow to cool in the oven for about 5 to 10 minutes. Transfer to a wire rack to cool completely before filling and serving.

(Continued)

VARIATIONS

Chouquettes: For a simple, tasty snack, sprinkle the unbaked puffs generously with pearl sugar right after the egg wash. No need to fill them with anything—just enjoy as-is, preferably the day they're made!

Craquelin-Topped: To add a professional look to your puffs, add a craquelin topping. This simple dough is placed on top of the puffs before baking and forms a pretty, crackly top while also helping the puffs rise evenly. To make craquelin, cream together 42 grams (3 tbsp) of softened unsalted butter and 50 grams (¼ cup) of light brown sugar until smooth. Add 50 grams (⅓ cup plus 1 tbsp) of all-purpose flour and mix to form a smooth dough. Place the dough between two sheets of parchment and roll until ⅛ inch (3 mm) thick. Freeze until ready to use. After piping out the puffs, use a round cookie cutter about the same diameter as the puffs to punch out rounds from the craquelin dough. Place on top of the puffs. Bake as directed.

Alternative Fillings: Instead of ice cream, fill the puffs with Vanilla-Almond Pastry Cream (page 162) or lightly sweetened whipped cream.

Alternative Toppings: Replace the Hot Fudge Sauce with Salted Caramel Sauce (page 164) or a dusting of icing sugar.

BAKER'S NOTES

You can assemble the puffs with the ice cream up to a day in advance—keep frozen until ready to serve.

The Hot Fudge Sauce can be prepared up to 2 weeks in advance. Store refrigerated in an airtight container. Reheat in the microwave before using.

HOT FUDGE SAUCE
28 g (2 tbsp) unsalted butter

160 g (⅔ cup) heavy cream

160 g (½ cup) light corn syrup

50 g (¼ cup) light or dark brown sugar

30 g (¼ cup) unsweetened Dutch-processed cocoa powder

1 tsp espresso powder

½ tsp kosher salt

170 g (1 cup) good-quality bittersweet chocolate (60–70% cacao), chopped

1 tsp pure vanilla extract

TO FINISH
2 pints vanilla ice cream

About 1 cup vanilla cake crumbs, from cake scraps or two cupcakes

30 g (¼ cup) rainbow sprinkles, plus more for decorating

Make the Hot Fudge Sauce: In a medium saucepan, whisk together the butter, cream, corn syrup, sugar, cocoa powder, espresso powder, and salt. Bring to a simmer over medium heat, stirring frequently. Once the mixture comes to a simmer, turn down the heat to low and continue simmering and stirring for about 5 minutes. It should thicken slightly. Remove from the heat and stir in the chocolate and vanilla. Transfer to a heatproof container and cool for about 15 to 20 minutes before using.

Assemble the Profiteroles: Transfer the ice cream to a medium bowl and allow to soften just slightly. Fold in the cake crumbs and sprinkles.

Cut the choux pastries in half horizontally. Place a scoop of ice cream in the bottom half of each puff. Replace the top halves and finish each with a drizzle of Hot Fudge Sauce and extra sprinkles. Serve immediately.

LIME CHEESECAKE ÉCLAIRS

MAKES ABOUT 15 ÉCLAIRS

LIME CURD
2 large eggs

2 large egg yolks

Pinch of salt

65 g (⅓ cup) granulated sugar

Zest of 2 limes

125 g (½ cup) lime juice, freshly squeezed

85 g (6 tbsp) unsalted butter, cubed

CHEESECAKE FILLING
250 g (1 block) cream cheese, at room temperature

65 g (⅓ cup) granulated sugar

Pinch of kosher salt

30 g (2 tbsp) sour cream, at room temperature

12 g (1½ tbsp) all-purpose flour

1 large egg, at room temperature

ÉCLAIR SHELLS
75 g (⅓ cup minus 1 tsp) water

75 g (⅓ cup minus 1 tsp) milk

70 g (5 tbsp) unsalted butter

1 tsp granulated sugar

½ tsp kosher salt

100 g (¾ cup plus 2 tsp) bread flour, sifted

150 g eggs (about 3 large), at room temperature and lightly beaten to combine

Icing sugar, for dusting

These éclairs are my play on key lime pie, with a zesty cream filling and a sprinkle of graham crackers on top. Making éclairs is a labor of love, but it's truly rewarding when you see these delightful confections come together. To break up the work, many of the components can be prepared ahead of time—the lime curd and cheesecake filling will keep for a week in the fridge, and the éclair shells can be baked a day in advance. Once filled, éclairs are best served within 6 hours before the pastry starts to soften.

Make the Lime Curd: Place a strainer over a heatproof container and set aside.

In a medium saucepan, whisk together the eggs, yolks, salt, sugar, lime zest, and lime juice until well blended.

Add the butter cubes. Cook over low heat, stirring constantly, until the butter is melted.

Increase the heat slightly to medium-low and continue cooking and stirring constantly until the curd thickens and coats the back of a spoon, about 5 minutes. Do not boil.

Press the curd through the strainer. Cool to room temperature, then cover and refrigerate until ready to use. The curd will thicken after chilling.

Make the Cheesecake Filling: Preheat the oven to 300°F (150°C) and lightly grease a 6-inch (15-cm) round cake pan. Combine the cream cheese, sugar, and salt in the bowl of a food processor. Pulse until smooth. Add the sour cream and flour and pulse until smooth. Add the egg and pulse just until combined. Scrape down the sides and fold the batter a few times to make sure it's well combined. Pour the batter into the prepared pan. Bake for about 20 to 25 minutes, or until the edges are puffed and set but the center is still quite loose. Cool completely on a wire rack, then cover and refrigerate until ready to use.

Make the Éclair Shells: Preheat the oven to 375°F (190°C) with a rack in the middle. Line a large baking sheet with parchment paper. Use a ruler to draw fifteen 4-inch (10-cm) lines, spaced 2 inches (5 cm) apart, to serve as a piping guide. Flip the parchment over so you don't get pen marks on your pastry.

Combine the water, milk, butter, sugar, and salt in a medium saucepan. Bring to a strong simmer over medium heat, stirring occasionally. As soon as the mixture is simmering, remove the pot from the heat and dump the flour in all at once. Stir vigorously with a wooden spoon or spatula until the flour is completely incorporated.

(Continued)

WHITE CHOCOLATE GLAZE
140 g (1 cup) white chocolate, chopped
64 g (¼ cup) heavy cream
40 g (2 tbsp) light corn syrup

TO FINISH
100 g (1 cup) graham cracker crumbs
Lime zest

Return the pot to low heat. Continue stirring vigorously until the mixture clears the side of the pot and forms a ball and a thin film forms on the bottom of the pot, about 2 to 3 minutes. The dough should be stiff enough that if you stick a small spoon in it, the spoon remains upright. Immediately transfer the dough to the bowl of a stand mixer fitted with the paddle attachment.

Mix the dough on low speed for 1 to 2 minutes to release the steam. An instant-read thermometer should read no warmer than 140°F (60°C).

When the dough has cooled sufficiently and with the mixer still on low, add about half of the beaten eggs in a slow, steady stream. Turn up the speed to medium and mix until the egg has been completely absorbed. Add more egg about 1 tablespoon at a time, mixing each addition in completely before adding more. When you've added most of the egg and the dough has taken on a glossy sheen, check the dough consistency—a finger dragged through it should leave a trough and a peak of dough should form where the finger is lifted. Once the dough passes this test, it's ready. You may not need all the egg—I usually have about 1 to 2 tablespoons left over.

Transfer the dough to a piping bag fitted with a large open star tip. Pipe the éclairs onto the prepared sheet, using the pre-drawn lines as guides. Once all the éclairs are piped, dust them with icing sugar.

Bake for about 30 to 40 minutes, or until the shells are completely golden brown and feel hollow when you pick one up. About 5 minutes before the shells are done, use a skewer or small knife to poke a small hole in each shell to help them crisp. Once the shells are done, turn the oven off, prop open the door, and allow to cool in the oven for about 5 to 10 minutes. Transfer to a wire rack to cool completely before filling and serving.

Make the White Chocolate Glaze: Place the chocolate in a heat-safe bowl. Microwave in 15-second increments, stirring after each burst. When the chocolate is almost all melted, allow the residual heat to complete the melting.

In a small saucepan, combine the cream and corn syrup. Heat on medium until just steaming. Remove from the heat. Pour the hot cream mixture over the melted chocolate in two parts, stirring between additions until smooth. Cool until just warm and a bit thick before using.

Assemble the Éclairs: In a medium bowl, whisk together the cheesecake filling with about 230 grams (1 cup) of the lime curd (you will have some curd left over). Transfer the filling to a piping bag and cut a small hole off the end.

Turn the cooled éclair shells over and use a small piping tip or paring knife to poke a small hole near each end. Fill each éclair with the lime cheesecake filling through the holes.

Carefully dip the top of each éclair in the glaze, allowing the excess to drip off. Use a clean finger to wipe away any drips. Garnish with the graham cracker crumbs and lime zest. Refrigerate until ready to serve. Éclairs are best served within 6 hours of filling.

VARIATIONS

Meringue Topping: Prepare a Vanilla Swiss Meringue Buttercream (page 79) but omit the butter. Once the meringue has cooled to room temperature, pipe or spoon the meringue on top of each éclair. Toast with a kitchen torch just before serving.

Strawberry Cheesecake: Omit the lime curd. Cut the éclairs in half lengthwise and fill the bottom with the cheesecake filling. Top with fresh sliced strawberries. Place the tops back on the éclairs and garnish with a swirl of whipped cream or a dusting of icing sugar.

Classic Éclairs: Fill the éclairs with Vanilla-Almond Pastry Cream (page 162). For the glaze, increase the cream to 160 grams (⅔ cup) and replace the white chocolate with dark (70 percent cacao) chocolate.

BAKER'S NOTES

I like to use bread flour in place of all-purpose flour when making choux pastry for éclairs, as the higher protein content creates a sturdier shell. Using an open star tip to pipe the shells helps them keep their shape and rise evenly in the oven.

MAPLE-GLAZED CRULLERS

MAKES ABOUT
15 CRULLERS

CRULLERS
125 g (½ cup) water
125 g (½ cup) milk
113 g (½ cup) unsalted butter
10 g (2 tsp) granulated sugar
¾ tsp kosher salt
167 g (1⅓ cups) bread flour, sifted
250 g eggs (about 5 large), at room temperature
Neutral vegetable oil, for frying

MAPLE GLAZE
150 g (1¼ cups) icing sugar, sifted
Pinch of kosher salt
40 g (2 tbsp) maple syrup
¼ tsp maple extract, or to taste (optional)
About 30 g (2 tbsp) milk or cream

Frying pâte à choux dough creates a whole new type of magic—namely French crullers. Crisp on the outside and pillowy soft on the inside, these crullers just may become your weekend breakfast of choice.

Make the Choux Pastry: Cut fifteen 3 x 3-inch (7.5 x 7.5-cm) squares of parchment paper and arrange on a sheet tray. Prepare a large piping bag fitted with a ½-inch (1.2-cm) star tip.

Combine the water, milk, butter, sugar, and salt in a medium saucepan. Bring to a strong simmer over medium heat, stirring occasionally. As soon as the mixture is simmering, remove the pot from the heat and dump the flour in all at once. Stir vigorously with a wooden spoon or spatula until the flour is completely incorporated.

Return the pot to low heat. Continue stirring vigorously until the mixture clears the side of the pot and forms a ball and a thin film forms on the bottom of the pot, about 2 to 3 minutes. The dough should be stiff enough that if you stick a small spoon in it, the spoon remains upright. Immediately transfer the dough to the bowl of a stand mixer fitted with the paddle attachment.

Mix the dough on low speed for 1 to 2 minutes to release the steam. An instant-read thermometer should read no warmer than 140°F (60°C).

When the dough has cooled sufficiently and with the mixer still on low, add about half of the beaten eggs in a slow, steady stream. Turn up the speed to medium and mix until the egg has been completely absorbed. Add more egg about 1 tablespoon at a time, mixing each addition in completely before adding more. When you've added most of the egg and the dough has taken on a glossy sheen, check the dough consistency—a finger dragged through it should leave a trough and a peak of dough should form where the finger is lifted. Once the dough passes this test, it's ready. You may not need all the egg—I usually have about 1 to 2 tablespoons left over. Transfer the dough to the prepared piping bag. Pipe circles about 2½ to 2¾ inches (6 to 7 cm) in diameter onto the parchment squares. Let sit uncovered while you heat the oil.

Fry and Glaze the Crullers: In a heavy-bottomed saucepan fitted with a candy thermometer, heat 3 to 4 inches (8 to 10 cm) of vegetable oil to 360 to 370°F (180 to 188°C). Place a cooling rack on a baking sheet lined with paper towels. Once the oil reaches temperature, carefully transfer two or three crullers, parchment side up, into the oil. (The parchment will release on its own—remove with tongs and discard). Fry for 6 to 8 minutes total, flipping every minute or so, until deeply golden. Remove from the oil and drain on the prepared rack. Repeat with remaining dough. Allow crullers to cool completely before glazing.

Prepare the Maple Glaze: Whisk together the icing sugar and salt in a medium bowl. Add the maple syrup and maple extract (if using) and whisk to combine. Add the milk 1 teaspoon at a time until you have a smooth, pourable glaze. Taste and add more maple extract, if desired. Dunk the cooled crullers into the glaze one at a time, allowing the excess to drip back into the bowl. Place on a wire rack to set before serving, about 10 minutes. Crullers are best enjoyed the day they're made.

VARIATIONS

Coffee-Glazed: In the glaze, replace the maple syrup with freshly brewed espresso or strong coffee.

Choux Beignets: Instead of piping the pâte à choux into rounds, simply drop spoonfuls of batter into the hot oil. Fry until deeply golden and puffed. Drain on paper towels and serve sprinkled with icing sugar.

Churros: Pipe 5- to 6-inch (13- to 15-cm) strips of dough into the hot oil, using a paring knife or kitchen shears to cut the dough as you are piping. Drain on paper towels and toss in cinnamon sugar (200 grams [1 cup] of granulated sugar mixed with 16 grams [2 tbsp] of ground cinnamon) while still warm.

BAKER'S NOTES

Make sure to completely cook your crullers and maintain an even oil temperature, as undercooked crullers will collapse after frying. I suggest frying one first to check the timings and temperature of your oil so you can adjust for the rest of the batch, if necessary.

LEFTOVERS

As a recipe tester and avid baker, I'm often left with little bits of ingredients and a few too many baked goods at the end of the day. What I can't give away or freeze, I try to repurpose into something new. I love the creative challenge of trying to resurrect scraps and give them a new, delicious second life.

In this chapter you'll find a few of my favorite ways to use up kitchen scraps such as half-eaten loaves of bread, stale cake, the ends of jam jars, and sourdough starter discard. I hope you'll use these recipes—such as Rum Raisin Bread Pudding (page 164) and Sourdough Granola Clusters (page 168)—as templates for creating your own delicious "scrap" bakes and to help you embrace leftovers as ingredients waiting to shine.

BLACK FOREST TRIFLE

MAKES 10–12 SERVINGS

VANILLA–ALMOND PASTRY CREAM
480 g (2 cups) whole milk

100 g (½ cup) granulated sugar, divided

Pinch of kosher salt

40 g (5 tbsp) cornstarch or custard powder

4 large egg yolks

1 tsp pure vanilla extract

½ tsp pure almond extract

28 g (2 tbsp) unsalted butter, cold and cubed

KIRSCH SIMPLE SYRUP
50 g (¼ cup) granulated sugar

60 g (¼ cup) water

14 g (1 tbsp) kirsch

WHIPPED CREAM
360 g (1½ cups) heavy cream, cold

120 g (½ cup) full-fat Greek yogurt or sour cream, cold

TO FINISH
600 grams (4 cups) chocolate cake or brownies, cubed

1½ batches Cherry Topping (page 90)

Chocolate shavings, for garnishing (optional)

Fresh cherries, for garnishing

Trifles are the superheroes of kitchen scraps, breathing new life into tired baked goods. They're the perfect home for slightly stale cake, brownies, or cookies, which can best soak up the flavors of added syrup, fruit, and cream. Here I've gone with the ever-popular Black Forest combo of cherries and chocolate, but you can (and should!) think of this as a basic template for concocting your own trifle masterpieces.

Make the Vanilla-Almond Pastry Cream: In a small saucepan off the heat, whisk together the milk, all but 13 grams (1 tbsp) of the sugar, and a pinch of salt. Place a strainer over a heat-safe jug or container.

In a medium bowl, whisk together the remaining sugar and the cornstarch. Pour in about 2 tablespoons of the milk mixture and whisk until smooth. (This helps keep the pastry cream from clumping.) Add the yolks and whisk until smooth.

Heat the milk mixture over medium heat until steaming. Remove from the heat. Pour the milk mixture in a slow, steady stream into the egg yolk mixture, whisking constantly. Scrape the custard mixture back into the saucepan and return to medium heat. Cook, whisking constantly, until the mixture thickens and large bubbles appear on the surface. Once the bubbles appear, turn the heat down to medium-low and continue whisking on the heat for 2 minutes.

Strain the pastry cream into the prepared jug or container. Whisk in the extracts and butter until combined. Press a piece of plastic wrap over the surface of the pastry cream and allow to cool to room temperature, then refrigerate until cold, at least 1 hour.

Make the Kirsch Simple Syrup: In a small saucepan, bring the sugar and water to a boil over medium-high heat. Reduce the heat to low and simmer for about 2 minutes. Remove from the heat and add the kirsch. Pour into a heatproof container and cool to room temperature.

Make the Whipped Cream: In the bowl of a stand mixer fitted with the whisk attachment, beat the cream and yogurt on low to combine. Raise the speed to medium-high and beat until soft peaks form.

Assemble the Trifle: Layer about one-third of the cake pieces in the bottom of an 2-quart (2-L) trifle dish (or similar sized serving dish, preferably clear). Brush the cake generously with the simple syrup. Spoon or pipe one-third of the pastry cream on top and smooth into an even layer. Top with one-third of the Cherry Topping, placing the cherries against the side of the bowl for the prettiest presentation. Top with one-third of the whipped cream. Repeat the layering two more times to fill the container. After the final layer of whipped cream, garnish with the chocolate shavings, if using, fresh cherries, and any stray cake crumbs. Refrigerate for about 1 hour before serving. The trifle is best served the day it's assembled.

VARIATIONS

Eton Mess: Replace the chocolate cake with sponge cake (page 92) or chiffon cake (page 87) and the Cherry Topping with about 680 grams (1½ lbs) of fresh strawberries, sliced and mixed with a couple large spoonfuls of sugar or strawberry jam. Add a layer of crushed meringues on top of each layer of whipped cream. Garnish with fresh strawberries. Serve right after assembling before the meringues soften.

Lemon-Raspberry: Replace the chocolate cake with Almond-Buttermilk Layer Cake (page 79) or chiffon cake (page 87) and the Cherry Topping with about 680 grams (1½ lbs) of fresh raspberries, sliced and mixed with a couple large spoonfuls of sugar or raspberry jam. Add the zest of 1 lemon to the milk when making the pastry cream and whisk in 45 grams (3 tbsp) of lemon juice with the extracts and butter. Fold 125 grams (½ cup) of Meyer Lemon Curd (page 79) into the whipped cream (add more to taste). Garnish with fresh raspberries.

Cookies-n-Cream: Omit the cherry layer. Omit the kirsch from the simple syrup. Omit the butter and almond extract from the pastry cream and whisk in 125 grams (½ block) of softened cream cheese into the pastry cream with the vanilla. Crush one package of OREO® cookies (about 30 cookies) or similar chocolate sandwich cookies into pieces of varying sizes. Right before assembling, fold in a handful of crushed cookies into the pastry cream. When assembling, layer the crushed cookies in place of the cherry layer, between the pastry cream and whipped cream. Garnish with any stray cake and cookie crumbs and serve with a drizzle of Hot Fudge Sauce (page 154).

BAKER'S NOTES

Adding Greek yogurt or sour cream to the whipped cream adds stability and tames the sweetness of the trifle. You can substitute plain or stabilized whipped cream (page 57) if you prefer. (I recommend stabilized if you plan on assembling the trifle more than 2 hours before serving.)

RUM RAISIN BREAD PUDDING

MAKES ONE
8 X 8–INCH
(20 X 20–CM) PAN

Humble bread pudding is the perfect solution for leftover bread. You can use any kind of bread you like, though egg-enriched breads such as challah or brioche yield especially custardy, indulgent results. This version is packed with raisins and a healthy dose of rum.

BREAD PUDDING
112 g (¾ cup) raisins

40 g (3 tbsp) dark rum

400 g (6 cups) bread, cut into ¾- to 1-inch (2- to 2.5-cm) cubes

130 g (⅔ cup) brown sugar, dark or light

½ tsp kosher salt

5 g (2 tsp) ground cinnamon

¼ tsp ground nutmeg

5 large eggs

10 g (2 tsp) pure vanilla extract

600 g (2½ cups) whole milk

Unsalted butter, softened, for greasing the pan

SALTED CARAMEL SAUCE
200 g (1 cup) granulated sugar

1 tsp fine sea salt

57 g (¼ cup) unsalted butter, at room temperature and cubed

120 g (½ cup) heavy cream, warm

1 tsp pure vanilla extract

Make the Bread Pudding: Preheat the oven to 325°F (160°C) with a rack in the middle. Combine the raisins and rum in a small bowl to soak.

Spread the bread cubes on a large baking sheet and toast in the oven until dry and lightly browned, about 15 to 20 minutes. Turn the pieces a couple of times during baking for even toasting. Transfer to a wire rack to cool slightly. Raise the oven temperature to 350°F (175°C).

In a large, wide bowl, whisk together the sugar, salt, cinnamon, and nutmeg. Add the eggs and vanilla and whisk until smooth. Add the milk and whisk until well combined. Add the raisins and toasted bread to the custard mixture and stir gently to combine, making sure all the bread gets covered. Let stand at room temperature for about 30 minutes, stirring occasionally, to let the bread absorb the custard.

Make the Salted Caramel Sauce: While the custard is sitting, in a medium (at least 3-quart [2.8-L]) heavy-bottomed, light-colored saucepan, sprinkle the sugar in an even layer. Place over medium heat. Once the sugar starts to melt around the edges, use a heatproof spatula to drag the melted parts toward the center of the pan. Continue dragging and swirling the pan to make sure the sugar is melting evenly and not scorching. If the mixture gets very lumpy and grainy, turn the heat down and stir as little as possible until the chunks melt.

As soon as the melted sugar turns the color of an old copper penny, remove it from the heat and add the salt and butter, stirring continuously. Be careful, as the mixture will bubble up! Return the pot to medium-low heat and whisk for about 1 minute or so until smooth and combined. Still continuously stirring, add the cream in a slow, steady stream. Continue stirring over medium-low heat for 1 to 2 minutes to thicken the sauce slightly.

Remove from the heat and stir in the vanilla. Transfer to a heat-safe container. You can use it immediately, or cool, cover, and refrigerate until ready to use.

Bake and Serve the Bread Pudding: Grease an 8 x 8-inch (20 x 20–cm) cake pan with the softened butter. Spoon the bread-custard mixture evenly into the pan and pour any un-absorbed custard over the top. Place the pan in a 9 x 13-inch (23 x 33–cm) baking pan or large roasting pan. Fill the larger pan with hot water so it comes up halfway up the sides of the 8 x 8-inch (20 x 20–cm) pan.

Bake until the center of the pudding is just set, about 40 to 50 minutes. A skewer inserted into the center should come out clean. Carefully lift the pan out of the water bath and transfer to a wire rack to cool for at least 15 minutes before serving. The pudding is best served warm, with a drizzle of Salted Caramel Sauce, but leftovers can be refrigerated up to 5 days and reheated in the microwave or enjoyed cold.

VARIATIONS

Savory: Omit the raisins, rum, sugar, spices, and vanilla. Mix in up to 226 grams (2 cups) of shredded cheese, roasted or sautéed veggies, and/or chopped, cooked meat such as ham or sausage, right before baking. You can also add in a handful of fresh herbs or 2 to 3 teaspoons of dried herbs and spices—such as dried mustard, paprika, oregano, thyme, sage, and tarragon—into the custard mixture before adding the toasted bread.

Apple: Peel and dice 2 to 3 baking apples. Melt 28 grams (2 tbsp) of butter in a large saucepan and sauté the apples with 12 grams (1 tbsp) of brown sugar and a pinch of cinnamon until tender. Add the apples to the custard mixture with the raisins and toasted bread.

Maple, Bourbon, and Pecan: Replace the rum with bourbon. Replace the brown sugar with 160 grams (½ cup) of maple syrup. Right before baking, sprinkle the top of the pudding with 90 grams (¾ cup) of chopped pecans.

Caramel Sauce Variations: For a boozy kick, stir in 30 grams (2 tbsp) of rum or bourbon with the vanilla. For an espresso caramel sauce, dissolve 4 grams (2 tsp) of espresso powder in the warm cream before adding to the caramel (do this before you start melting the sugar).

BAKER'S NOTES

For an extra-rich pudding, replace some or all of the milk with half-and-half, or use equal parts whole milk and heavy cream.

BOSTOCK

FRANGIPANE
98 g (7 tbsp) unsalted butter, at room temperature

100 g (½ cup) granulated sugar

½ tsp kosher salt

2 large eggs, at room temperature

10 g (2 tsp) pure vanilla extract

100 g (1 cup) almond flour

15 g (2 tbsp) all-purpose flour

SIMPLE SYRUP
100 g (½ cup) granulated sugar

120 g (½ cup) water

30 g (2 tbsp) dark rum or bourbon (optional)

TO FINISH
8 thick slices challah, brioche, or enriched white bread, preferably day-old

85 g (⅔ cup) sliced almonds

Icing sugar, for garnishing

Confession: I often make challah or brioche just so I can indulge in bostock, which is basically an almond croissant except made with bread. Day-old bread is ideal for this pastry—you want the slices a little dry so they can soak up a good amount of simple syrup; if you don't have day-old bread, toast fresh bread slices in a 300°F (150°C) oven until dry to the touch. All the elements can be prepped in advance (you can even assemble the unbaked pastries and refrigerate, covered, overnight), making bostock an excellent option for weekend brunch or feeding a crowd.

Make the Frangipane: Beat together the butter, sugar, and salt until smooth. Beat in the eggs one at a time, followed by the vanilla. Fold in the flours until evenly combined. Refrigerate for about 30 to 60 minutes to firm up and allow the flavors to meld. (Frangipane can be stored in the fridge for up to 5 days or frozen for up to 3 months; bring to spreadable room temperature before using.)

Make the Simple Syrup: Combine the sugar and water in a small saucepan and bring to a simmer over medium heat, stirring until the sugar has dissolved. Turn off the heat and stir in the rum, if using. Pour the syrup into a heat-safe container and cool to room temperature. Refrigerate until ready to use.

Assemble and Bake the Bostock: Preheat the oven to 375°F (190°C) with a rack in the middle. Line a baking sheet with parchment paper or a silicone mat.

Arrange the bread slices on the prepared baking sheet. Brush each slice generously with the simple syrup until they are well soaked. Top each slice with about 45 grams (3 tbsp) of frangipane, followed by a sprinkling of slivered almonds.

Bake until the frangipane is puffed and golden on the edges, about 15 to 20 minutes. Cool slightly on a wire rack, then dust the slices with icing sugar right before serving. Bostock is best enjoyed the day it's made.

VARIATIONS

Jam Layer: For an extra layer of flavor, add 15 grams (1 tbsp) of jam or preserves between the simple syrup and frangipane. Something tart (such as Rhubarb Jam, page 42) works especially nicely to complement the richness of the frangipane.

Customize Your Frangipane: Substitute some, or all, of the almond flour with another type of nut flour or finely ground nuts, such as pecans, hazelnuts, pistachios, or walnuts. You can also substitute the granulated sugar for 100 grams (5 tbsp) of honey, and swap out the vanilla or almond extract for an alcohol such as rum, bourbon, or brandy.

Lemon-Blackberry: Replace all, or part of, the water in the simple syrup with freshly squeezed lemon juice and omit the rum or bourbon. When assembling, press a few fresh blackberries (halved if large) into the frangipane before sprinkling with the slivered almonds.

Almond Croissants: You can use these same ingredients with day-old croissants to make twice-baked almond croissants. Split the croissants horizontally and brush the insides with the simple syrup. Spread the frangipane on the bottom halves of the croissants, reserving about 120 grams (½ cup) for the tops of the croissants. Close the croissants, then spread the remaining frangipane over the tops of the croissants and sprinkle with the sliced almonds. Bake as directed.

SOURDOUGH GRANOLA CLUSTERS

MAKES ABOUT
1,250 GRAMS (8 CUPS)

200 g (scant 1 cup) 100% hydration sourdough starter, fed or unfed

60 g (¼ cup) water

60 g (scant ½ cup) all-purpose flour

60 g (¼ cup plus 2 tsp) light or dark brown sugar

55 g (¼ cup) neutral vegetable oil, such as grapeseed or canola

70 g (3½ tbsp) honey or maple syrup

320 g (3½ cups) rolled oats (not quick)

140 g (1 cup) whole raw almonds

30 g (¼ cup) unsweetened shredded coconut

70 g (½ cup) mixed seeds, such as sesame, flax, millet, and poppy

½ tsp kosher salt

200 g (1½ cups) dried fruit, chopped if large

My Monday routine includes making a batch of this granola, which is one of my go-to ways for using up leftover sourdough starter. The starter helps bind the oat mixture to create a crunchy and "clustery" granola—my favorite kind. This recipe is quite forgiving—if you keep to the general wet and dry ingredient proportions, you can be flexible with the add-ins. Try subbing in puffed grains for some of the nuts, or experimenting with other flaked grains for part of the oats.

In a medium bowl, mix together the sourdough starter, water, flour, and sugar until evenly combined. Cover and let sit at room temperature until bubbly and expanded, about 3 to 4 hours (or up to 8 hours).

Preheat the oven to 300°F (150°C) with racks in the upper and lower thirds and line two baking sheets with parchment paper or silicone mats.

Whisk the oil and honey into the sourdough starter mixture until well combined. In a large bowl, mix together oats, almonds, coconut, mixed seeds, and salt. Scrape the wet ingredients over the dry and mix with a flexible spatula until evenly combined.

Divide the mixture between the two prepared baking sheets, pressing down into thin, even layers. Bake for 40 to 50 minutes or until golden brown and firm, rotating the trays top to bottom and front to back halfway through baking. After about 30 minutes of baking, use a heatproof spatula to carefully turn over sections of the granola for even browning.

Transfer the pans to wire racks to cool completely, then break the granola into pieces and mix in the dried fruit. Store in an airtight container for up to 2 weeks.

VARIATIONS

Pumpkin Spice: Add 120 grams (½ cup) of pumpkin puree and 5 grams (2 tsp) of pumpkin pie spice with the oil and honey or maple syrup. Replace the almonds with pecans. Use pumpkin seeds for all, or part of, the mixed seeds.

Nut Butter: Replace the vegetable oil with 55 grams (¼ cup) of smooth nut butter.

Chocolate-Cherry: Add 60 grams (½ cup) of Dutch-processed cocoa powder with the rolled oat mixture. Replace the dried fruit mix-ins with 85 grams (½ cup) of semi-sweet chocolate chips and 140 grams (1 cup) of dried cherries.

SOURDOUGH LAVASH *and* GRISSINI

MAKES ONE (13 X 18–INCH
[33 X 46–CM]) BAKING SHEET
OF CRACKERS

100 g (scant ½ cup) 100% hydration
sourdough starter, fed or unfed

10 g (2 tsp) olive oil

10 g (1½ tsp) honey

50 g (⅓ cup plus 1 tbsp) all-purpose
flour

½ tsp kosher salt

Assorted seeds, such as poppy, flax,
or sesame (optional)

Flaky salt for topping (optional)

Crackers are one of my favorite ways to use up sourdough discard—they keep incredibly well and are extremely adaptable to different flavorings and shapes. Roll the dough thin to make a large sheet of lavash crackers, which you can break apart after baking to make beautiful shards; or roll it a little thicker and cut into strips for crisp *grissini* (breadsticks). Both make beautiful additions to *charcuterie* boards or cheese plates.

Stir together the starter, oil, and honey until combined. Add the flour and salt and mix with a spatula until it forms into a rough dough. Knead for 3 to 5 minutes, or until the ingredients are well combined and the dough is smooth. It should be a medium-firm consistency and not sticky. If it is sticky, add flour 1 teaspoon at a time until smooth. If it is dry, add water 1 teaspoon at a time until hydrated. Transfer to an oiled container.

Ferment the dough at room temperature until it is doubled in size, about 3 to 4 hours.

To Make Lavash Crackers: When the dough is nearly ready, preheat the oven to 400°F (200°C), using a baking stone if you have one. Turn the dough onto a silicone mat or piece of parchment paper cut to fit a 13 x 18–inch (33 x 46–cm) baking sheet.

Roll the dough into a rectangle as thinly and evenly as possible. It should be almost paper thin. If you want to add seeds, sprinkle them evenly over the surface of the dough and use a rolling pin to gently press them into the surface.

Transfer the dough, still on the silicone mat or parchment, to a baking sheet. Pierce the surface all over with a fork to keep it from puffing in the oven. Mist with water and sprinkle on the flaky salt, if desired.

Bake for 10 to 15 minutes, rotating the sheet halfway through baking, until browned and crisp. Cool completely on a wire rack, then break into shards. Store in an airtight container for up to 2 months.

To Make Grissini: When the dough is nearly ready, preheat the oven to 350°F (175°C) and line a baking sheet with a silicone mat or parchment paper. If you'd like to coat your grissini with seeds, place the seeds on a plate or small baking sheet.

On a clean work surface, roll the dough into a rectangle about ¼ inch (6 mm) thick. Cut the dough into even strips into desired thickness (I like ¼-inch [6-mm]-thick strips). Roll them one by one in the bed of seeds, if desired, then transfer to the prepared sheet.

Bake until dry and crisp, about 30 to 40 minutes (the time can vary wildly depending on the size of your grissini). Cool completely on a wire rack, then store in an airtight container or jar.

VARIATIONS

Herb: Add 1 to 2 teaspoons of dried herbs such as thyme, tarragon, rosemary, and/or oregano to the dough while mixing.

Whole-Grain: Replace the all-purpose flour with a whole-grain flour such as whole-wheat, spelt, einkorn, or rye flour.

Parmesan and Black Pepper: Add 25 grams (¼ cup) of finely grated Parmesan and ¼ teaspoon of freshly ground black pepper while mixing. Roll to ⅛ inch (3 mm) and bake at 350°F (175°C) for about 25 to 30 minutes, or until golden and crisp. (I like to roll this dough a little thicker and bake it at a lower temperature to keep the cheese from scorching.)

acknowledgments

To My Parents: Thank you for always encouraging me to pursue my dreams, for teaching me the importance of sharing a good meal with others, and for your constant wise counsel and godly example.

To Steve, Dan, Joe, and Tim: Thank you for enthusiastically encouraging this book from the start. We've come a long way since writing our pretend restaurant menus.

To My Toronto Family—Mom and Dad Tam, Mary, and Andrew: Thank you for welcoming me into your family and for your constant support and generosity. Thank you for always offering to watch the kids so I could get some extra writing done; I couldn't have written this book without your help!

To My Family at Toronto Holy Word Church: Thank you for your encouragement and for being my recipe guinea pigs. Your fellowship and friendship are invaluable.

To Diana Muresan: Thank you for bringing your creative vision to this project and for the care you poured into every image. You made each recipe look more beautiful than I could have on my own.

To the Page Street Publishing Team: Thank you for taking a chance on me and for patiently guiding this newbie through the whole cookbook-writing process.

To My Team of Recipe Testers: Lindsay Branch, Mimi Chau, Trinity Cheng, Bernice Chung, Jenna Clarke, Erin Clarkson, Elena Efthimiou, Brooke Hanson, Jacqueline Ho, Janelle Ho, Eunhee Jo, Molly Kalkenstein, Megan Katsumi, Royce Li, Heather MacMillan, Victoria Ng, Quinn O'Keefe, Liz Overton, Jannica Quach, Caryn Sherbet, Mina Sidd, Kerry Sutherland, and Radka Tam. Thank you for helping ensure these recipes would be clear and work in kitchens other than my own.

To My Teachers: I am indebted to my major music teachers—Alison Austin, Heidi Lehwalder, Judy Loman, and Willard Schultz. Skills I learned through years of music lessons—patience, memorization, attention to detail, how to practice, and artistic taste, among others—are also invaluable in the kitchen.

To My Blog Readers and Followers: Thank you for trying my recipes, sending me photos of your bakes, and enthusiastically supporting my work. This book wouldn't have been possible without you.

To Marcus, Hannah, and Isabelle: Thank you for being my most honest taste-testers, sous chefs, and biggest fans. Thank you for reminding me that sprinkles do make a lot of things better.

To David: Thank you for everything you have done behind the scenes—late-night ingredient runs, countless loads of dishes, child-wrangling, taste-testing, and so much more. But thank you most for your unwavering support, level-headed encouragement, and confidence in me. I love you.

about the author

Ruth Mar Tam is a self-taught baker and the blogger behind cooktildelicious.com. A native of Seattle, she currently lives in the greater Toronto area with her husband, David, and their three children.

index